DO WE HAVE
AN IMMORTAL SOUL?

OREST STOCCO

DO WE HAVE AN IMMORTAL SOUL?

ISBN 978-0-9920112-6-0

Edited by Penny Lynn Cates

Cover Design by Penny Lynn Cates

"There is nothing but the self and God."

THE KEYS OF JESHUA
Glenda Green

Table of Contents

1. The Question

Do we have an immortal soul? Some people believe we do, and some people don't. I do; and I would like to tell you why. But where to begin?

Robert H. Hopcke wrote in *There Are No Accidents, Synchronicity and the Stories of Our Lives,* "Even the road to nowhere leads somewhere." So it doesn't matter where I begin, really; I know that I will get there eventually, because I trust that the divine law of synchronicity will bring all the relevant variables of my life together in happy coincidence to resolve this nagging question...

The idea for this narrative essay came to me the other morning when Penny and I were having our morning coffee. Penny joins me for coffee every morning in my writing den, and we talk about our dreams and whatever comes to mind.

It's a wonderful way to begin the day, because we start the day off together. She goes off to work, and I stay home and write because I've been off work ever since I had open heart surgery. I'm very thankful for Penny's love.

After we shared our dreams I told her about the idea for a new book I had been strongly nudged to write on the nature of the self. "A personal essay, actually," I explained; and I went on to tell her that the idea was set free by a You Tube video I had just seen, a revealing dialogue between lay monk Brother Wayne Teasdale and philosopher Ken Wilber. It was titled The Mystic Heart (Part 1: The Supreme Identity), which I watched with eager anticipation because I was currently reading Wayne Teasdale's book *The Mystic Heart* and I had just recently read Ken Wilber's *Grace and Grit*, the true story of his wife's five year ordeal with cancer, his book *Eye to Eye, The Quest for the New Paradigm*, and had just started reading his very ambitious book *A Brief History of Everything.*

Both men believed that we do not have an autonomous self; meaning, an individual, immortal soul. Brother Wayne explained to Wilber that he perceived the self to be a point of divine light. He asked Wilber to imagine a huge board that stood between existence and the Godhead. The board is full of tiny holes, and the light of the Godhead shines through these holes. The divine light of the Godhead that shines through the holes is who we are. These are his exact words that I transcribed from the video:

"We are the little points of light, but we are not autonomous in ourselves. We are that light. Or as Eckhart would say, you are God, he, she, or it (is) God, I am God; but God is not you, he, she, it or they. But that infinite light, we are ontologically that in the deepest part of ourselves. That's all we can be."

I strongly disagree. I don't disagree with his belief that we are all points of divine light; I disagree with his belief that that's all we can be. I believe that we are all points of divine light, but I also believe that we are points of divine light that evolve through life into autonomous souls with our own distinct identity; and how I came to this belief is the subject of this very personal essay...

2. The Journey Begins

I was born Roman Catholic, and despite the fact that I was an altar boy who seriously entertained the prospect of becoming a priest one day I left the Church at an early age to look for a path better suited to my spiritual needs. What my spiritual needs were, I could not articulate at the time; but I knew that my Roman Catholic faith did not satisfy them, and I suffered the unbearable anguish of a trapped soul.

In grade twelve I read Somerset Maugham's novel *The Razor's Edge*, and I was so moved by his hero Larry Darrel that I was inspired to become a truth seeker like him and began my own quest for the meaning and purpose of life.

Larry Darrel was a pilot in WW1, and during a "dogfight" in the sky his pilot friend saw that Larry was in trouble and sacrificed his life to save Larry's. His friend's sacrifice marked Larry for life, and after the war he dropped out of life and went on a spiritual quest to look for the meaning and purpose of life.

I don't remember exactly when it happened, whether it was before I read *The Razor's Edge* or after, but I had another experience in grade twelve that set my soul ablaze for my spiritual quest; I wrote a narrative poem called "Noman."

"Noman" was set free from the depths of my creative unconscious by the medieval English morality play *The Summoning of Everyman* (simply called *Everyman*) that I had just read several days before I wrote my poem; but so possessed was I by the *daemonic* spirit of my creative impulse when I wrote my poem that all these years later it inspired my book *The Summoning of Noman, The True Story of My Parallel Life*.

"Noman" was a very strange poem that erupted out of the deepest recesses of my unconscious self like a volcano of molten effluvia. Like Everyman, Noman is summoned to God for a reckoning; and like Everyman, he's found wanting. But why was my poem called "Noman"? Who is Noman?

In my poem, I am Noman; but it took many years before I came to see that Noman was what C. G. Jung, the eminent Swiss psychologist who broke away from Sigmund Freud to start his own branch of analytical psychology, called the *shadow*; which is the repressed, unconscious side of the human personality.

Noman not only symbolized the dark *shadow* side of my personality, but the *archetypal shadow* of every personality in the world, just as Everyman symbolized every person in the world. **Noman was Everyman's *shadow***; and in my reckoning with God I was asked to return God's "fish's scale," which I learned many years later to be my lost soul.

In my poem, I was given three days by God to find my lost soul in the "abyss with four corners" (meaning, the four corners of the world: North, South, East, and West), but I only had one day to search each corner of the abyss. This meant that if I failed to find my lost soul within my allotted three days, one corner of the abyss would not be searched and I would fail to return God's "fish's scale."

I failed; and God condemned me to the fourth corner of the abyss to find my lost soul. And as I fell from Heaven into the fourth corner of the abyss I shouted the only words of my poem that I can still remember:

> *"Open you vile, voracious, loveable sweet whore!*
> *God, why hast thou forsaken me?*

I was a teenager. I was a virgin. Where in God's name did that come from? The depths of those two lines were so profound that they reverberated throughout my entire life like the echoes of a cracked bell, and not until I had seven past-life regressions just a few years ago and was brought back to my sexually debauched and morally depraved *"le salaud de Paris"* lifetime in Paris, France in the 17th Century did I grasp the karmic significance of my poem "Noman."

3. The Discovery

Reincarnation. This is an ancient belief that we live multiple lives. Our soul, according to one interpretation of this belief, is reborn into another body when we die; and according to another interpretation, which is essentially Buddhist in perspective, the non-autonomous "point of light" is born again and again in a new body. This poses a real problem for the concept of the self, which took me many years to resolve.

I discovered reincarnation in my teens. It was as much of a shock to my psyche as two women kissing and making love, which I discovered in one of my older brother's adult novels. I couldn't believe what I read; either the lesbian love scene, or the belief that when we die we are reborn into another body. I was much too Catholic.

But the world was opening up to me, and my paradigm began to shift; and I became an insatiable reader. In grade eight I read a book a day. I had a ravenous hole in my soul that could not be filled no matter how much I read, and over the years I accumulated a personal library of thousands of books, most of the books related to my search.

I was a young and naïve Catholic in high school, and reincarnation was as foreign to me as lesbian sex; but once I got over my initial shock it excited my curiosity, and I dared to step outside my Christian paradigm. That's how I discovered Edgar Cayce, the amazing psychic who did more to introduce the western world to reincarnation than any other person with his thousands of past-life readings and healings. Some even consider Edgar Cayce to be the true founder of the New Age Movement. I came upon Edgar Cayce through Jess Stearn's best-selling book *Edgar Cayce: The Sleeping Prophet*.

Strangely enough however, life had prepared me for my discovery of reincarnation; because in my teens I had dreams that revealed at least four of my past lives. I did not know that these were past-life recollection dreams, but I *knew* that the person in my dreams was me in another body in another time.

In one dream I'm a fish monger in London, England. I don't know what century it was, but I was definitely a fish monger pulling my cart through the cobbled streets shouting "KIPPERS! FILLETS! KIPPERS!" The sights and smells were so palpable and real that the very memory brings me back there.

In another dream I'm a North American Indian. This dream made such an impression upon me that I could rest my case for reincarnation upon this dream alone; but there was much more to come in my quest for my true self.

I'm a young man in this dream, and I've been called by the tribal council to go through my rite of passage into manhood; but I have witnessed this rite of passage several times, and it terrifies me. I don't have the courage to go through with it.

It's a very painful rite of passage, not unlike what Richard Harris had to go through in the movie *A Man Called Horse;* but I have two choices: I can leave the tribal village and live on my own to build up enough courage to go through my rite into manhood, or I can stay and be relegated to a life that would be less than a dog's. I would be treated with absolute disdain. Even the squaws of the village would show me less respect than they gave to the dogs. There were two men in our village who were treated this way.

I chose to leave the village and live in the wilderness. I am provided with whatever I need to forage my keep—my bow and arrows, knife, tomahawk, spear, and pelts to keep me warm; and I manage to survive one whole winter on my own. To my private shame however, my mother snuck food out to me several times throughout the brutal winter, which was enough to keep my body and soul together; but come springtime I returned to the village and was initiated into manhood.

I grew to become chief of my village. My tribal name was Bear Claw, and I was given this name because I had killed a bear with nothing but my knife. The bear clawed my face, which left a permanent scar (hence my name), and I was chief of my tribe as long as I had the power to rule.

I was challenged twice by young warriors who thirsted for power, and they paid with their life. I attributed my victories to my talisman, the bear's claw that hung from my waist; which, according to our village shaman, endowed me with the power of the Bear Spirit. I was a hard chief, but respected by my people.

In my third dream I'm in Athens in ancient Greece. I'm a statesman, and I'm speaking to the men that have been called in from the outskirts to help defend our noble city from an impending invasion. The men have all been armed and assembled, and I say to them: "Remember who you are. When you kill, do not kill with savagery; but with the dignity of your noble bearing. We are not savages. We are Athenians, and we must defend our way of life—"

Years later I read Jess Stearn's book *The Search for the Soul: Psychic Lives of Taylor Caldwell*, and I knew that one day I would write a book on my own past lives; and when Penny and I moved to Georgian Bay ten or twelve years later I met a past-life regressionist by "chance" and had seven past-life regressions, and in my third regression I was brought back to my lifetime in Athens in ancient Greece.

I was born into a noble family, and my name was Phaedrus; and I was a student of the mystic philosopher Pythagoras before I went into politics to serve our noble city state. I studied the secret doctrine of reincarnation for eight years with Pythagoras in Italy, and I went on to teach the secret doctrine in secret for thirty years before retiring from my lifetime of service to my beloved Athens. I will never forget Pythagoras. He was truly a master of mystic wisdom, and he altered the course of my karmic destiny which I make specific reference to in my novel *The Waking Dream*.

But the dream that had the most powerful effect upon me was the dream of my past lifetime in southern Georgia, USA. My name was Solomon, and I was a black slave condemned to do my master's bidding. I ran away twice from the plantation; and the second time that I got caught I was made an example of for the rest of the slaves: every Sunday morning I was stripped and whipped.

The lashes on my back never healed enough from week to week, and eventually my wounds got infected and I died in anguish; but what made this life so memorable was what I experienced during one of my final whippings.

I would not surrender my will to the master's whip, and one Sunday morning after a dozen lashes or so one lash set me free from myself, and I knew that no matter how much they whipped my body and controlled my wretched life that they could never be the master of my soul. I was as certain of that as I was that God had made the earth and sky.

This was my first realization that I had an immortal soul independent of my body, and that in my soul I was free. I died shortly after this realization, but I had accomplished what I had been born to accomplish; *to awaken to my own immortal soul.*

4. What Does The Brothers Karamazov Have to Do with It?

The Soul and Christianity. Christianity does not believe that our immortal soul pre-exists our mortal human body; Christianity believes that our immortal soul is created at the moment of human conception, and that we only live one lifetime.

This is what I was brought up to believe. I did not know about reincarnation. It was totally absent from my realm of knowledge. We lived one life, and Jesus Christ died on the cross to wash away the stain of Original Sin that we all inherit from our first parents Adam and Eve, and that was it; end of story.

As irony would have it however, when I was well into my quest for my true self I discovered that an early Christian sect called the Gnostics believed in the secret doctrine of reincarnation; but the Church Fathers condemned the Gnostics as heretics, and the secret doctrine was kept secret, but for the wrong reasons. Not because it wasn't true; but because the very concept of living more than one lifetime undermined Christian doctrine.

I learned that the secret doctrine of reincarnation was expunged from Christianity at the First Council of Nicaea in 325 A.D. that had been convened by the Roman Emperor Constantine, who wanted to bring all the separate factions of Christianity under one roof. Whether or not it was at the behest of Emperor Constantine, all the Christian bishops that had been assembled in Nicaea decreed Christ to be the one true God in deity with the Father, and only through Jesus Christ could one be saved; and all references to reincarnation were removed from the Gospels.

With reincarnation gone, the only way to salvation was through Jesus Christ; which gave Christianity all the power it needed to control the masses. And as incredible as it may seem, to this very day—despite the advent of the Internet and Google—the vast majority of Christians are still ignorant of reincarnation; which is why it came as such a shock to me to learn about reincarnation so early in my life.

I had no choice but to leave the Church. I had outgrown my Roman Catholic faith and needed a new path. But outgrowing one's faith and leaving it are two different things entirely. Many Christians outgrow their faith but cannot leave it. They stay trapped and suffer the spiritual anguish of bad faith; like the United Church minister that I met one morning a number of years ago while painting the Catholic priest's residence next door to the minister's manse in my hometown of Nipigon, Northwestern Ontario.

The minister was newly retired, but he was filling in until they could get a new minister for the United Church in our community. He had just moved into the manse the day before, and he stepped out the back door early the next morning with his coffee.

He saw me on my ladder and bid me good morning. I deliberately struck up a conversation, because I was curious to know how he felt about the burning issue of the day in the United Church of allowing gays into the ministry.

He told me that the United Church was very open-minded, and then he informed me that he himself was what he called an "agnostic Christian." Startled, I replied: "That's a contradiction in terms. How can you be an agnostic and a Christian at the same time? To be a Christian is to know God through His only Begotten Son Jesus, and an agnostic by definition cannot know God. I don't follow your logic."

He then informed me that he did not believe that Jesus was the Son of God, and I bluntly replied: "Then what are you still doing in the ministry? I would have thought that Christ's divinity would be a prerequisite for being a Christian minister."

Scratching for ground, he tried to justify his position by making some reference to Dostoevsky's novel *The Brothers Karamazov*; but it was painfully obvious that he didn't believe in what he was telling me, and he squirmed like a worm.

Upon reflection, I realized that he did not leave his ministry because he was getting a free ride in life. He had a house to live in, a car to drive, and though modest a monthly salary. Such was the face of his bad faith, and although I ran into him a few more times in the course of the next few years, we never struck up another conversation.

5. The Coiled Serpent

I had a sexual experience in my early twenties that shocked my conscience awake and catapulted me into my spiritual quest for my true self. Out of shame and guilt, I sold my pool hall and vending machine business and fled to France.

One night in the beautiful Alpine city of Annecy where I was living, I accidentally opened up the chakra at the base of my spine while meditating and awakened the kundalini energy. I was reading a book on meditation, and I focused my mind on a maple leaf that I had picked up and studied intensely as I waited for my friend's two young daughters to get out of school so I could walk them home.

That evening I observed the leaf's beauty and texture and aroma, and then I imagined myself enter the tiny aperture at the stem of the leaf which I called "the golden gate" and go up each vein to its extremity, and I imagined myself becoming one with the leaf.

I don't know how long I did this for, but when it happened it was so dramatic that I had to record the experience on the only available paper that I had handy—the blank front and back covers of the novel that I was reading; *Wuthering Heights*, by Emily Bronte. I dated my experience: October 21, 1968. I was twenty-three years old.

I had no idea what I was doing, and I certainly did not have the appropriate vocabulary to express my kundalini experience. I don't think I had even come across the word kundalini, let alone know what it meant. Nonetheless, this experience was to dramatically change my life. I haven't changed a single word of my experience, because I want my raw and emotionally confusing kundalini awakening to speak for itself.

I don't know what synchronistic relevance this had to the novel *Wuthering Heights* (perhaps my kundalini awakening had literally set free my *archetypal shadow* as Emily Bronte had creatively set free her *archetypal shadow* in Heathcliff), but here's what I recorded in the inside blank covers of this classic story of unrequited love:

Tonight I think I have experienced meditation in its truest form. How and why I will explain. I had been reading a book, Concentration: An Approach to Meditation; *and in it I read that to meditate one must so to speak become harmonious with what he is meditating on. The example it gave was a flower. It said to observe the flower very carefully the next time you passed a flower. To stop, pick up the flower, observe it, feel it, smell it, note its colors, its texture, everything about the flower, and then when you want to meditate, in your moment of tranquility to pick that beautiful little flower as your object of meditation.*

Well, I did this; only with a leaf. By sheer accident yesterday when I was waiting for the kids to come out of school I happened to pick up a fallen maple leaf. I fiddled around with it for a while, and then what I had read about the flower came to me, and I observed the leaf as closely as I could. I noted its color, its texture, its size, shape, and even its odor, and the conclusion I came to was that it was beautiful. It really was beautiful. I did not want to throw it away. I wanted to keep it forever and forever. I wanted it. I cherished it. I loved it. I loved a leaf! But then I thought of the absurdity of it all, and still I clung to it.

I did not want to throw it away, and I did not until the young girls came out of school, for it was then that being forced by the sheer reality of our difference, because as I gave Sabrina and Patricia a kiss on the cheek I let it slip hesitantly from my hand and quickly grasped the girls' hands, one on each side, to get in touch with real people, real existence, and yet I could not stop feeling that that beautiful little leaf did have an existence of its own and that I had come to realize it. Now I believe it has. Here is what happened:

I was sitting alone reading, and it was very quiet except for the ticking of a clock. Then the idea struck me to try meditation on that leaf I had so perspicaciously observed. I must note here that when I observed the leaf it was smooth and waxy on one side and the other was not so smooth owing to the veins which projected from the main stem to all the extremities of the leaf. And the stem was fine and thin on its attachment but thickened progressively as it neared its creator, and when the wind had separated it how there remained a slight yet noticeable hole which I made a note of recollecting at the time because if ever I was to meditate on that leaf my existence would become harmonious with its existence via this golden gate, and so I assumed the position directed in the book to sit with my feet flat on the floor, my back as straight as comfort would allow, my hands resting on my knees, and my head straight and my eyes looking straight ahead, and slowly I began to meditate on the leaf.

I began my meditation by observing first its size, shape, and form, and I viewed it mentally from all angles, up, down, sideways, frontwards, backwards, and then I observed its color, texture, and odor; then all my observations were meditated upon simultaneously with a center of concentration upon the golden gate. I concentrated and concentrated, and as I did so I repeated such lines to myself: "How beautiful you are. I want to be you. I want my existence to be your existence. I want that we should be one and the same. We will be harmonious." And as I repeated these lines I pictured my "self," my existence (and it was not normal, for I pictured my existence as shapeless, formless, without creation, as though it was the "me" of me) enter the golden gate slowly, very slowly, and as I began to enter my back began to stiffen, and the deeper my existence went into the existence of the leaf the more rigid my back became and the lighter my head felt, and the lighter it felt the more it began to float, and as the "me" of me entered into the veins of the leaf I felt a certain physical levitation which was climaxed by a certain mental euphoria as the "me" of me touched every extremity of the leaf and became one and the same as the "it" of it.

I consciously felt, for I had not by any means lost my powers of reason for I was still conscious of what was going on because deep down somewhere I knew it was just an experiment, but nevertheless I consciously felt a symbiosis, a union with the "me" and the "it" united to make "one". This had such a physical effect on me that the stiffening of my back and the weightlessness of my head, as though it wanted to leave the body and float away somewhere, snapped me into, so to speak, the materialistic reality of it all that it sent a momentary chill through me and in order for me to get back into the swing of things I decided to relinquish the experiment, but I did this carefully also.

I slowly withdrew my existence—the "me" from the "it" via the same means of entry, and curiously enough as I did this my back began to lose the rigidity it experienced and my head the

13

weightlessness, and the further the "me" withdrew the more normal I became until when the "me" was completely removed and inharmonious with the "it" I felt the way I had begun my meditation, tranquil, phlegmatic, yet somehow thwarted.

It embarrasses me to reveal this, but it speaks to my state of mind. I was in a foreign country. I did not speak French well at all. I was very much in the throes of cultural shock (not to mention psychological shock from my brutally awakened conscience), and then I compound my confusion with this remarkable experience; but now that I recall my kundalini awakening, I'm amazed that I failed to write down the most important aspect of my experience—the raising of the "coiled serpent."

The "coiled serpent" is the metaphor used to describe the kundalini energy that is released when the chakara at the base of the spine has been opened; and I can distinctly remember how a tiny bubble floated up the canal of my spine all the way to my head. It felt like a "serpent" crawling up my back through my spine; a strange, tickling sensation.

Although I had absolutely no idea what happened to me that night, I began to feel the fierce energy of the kundalini as it set my mind on fire; and I won't hesitate to confess now that it took a minimum of ten years to tame the "serpent fire."

It nearly drove me out of my mind…

6. My Big Dream in Annecy, France

I don't know when exactly, but not long after my kundalini awakening I had a dream that spoke to the enigmatic nature of the self of man; but of course I had absolutely no idea that that's what it spoke to, and it took many years before I was able to work out the symbolic meaning of this phenomenal dream.

In my dream I left my body and entered into the mind of every person in the world—man, woman, and child; and I took every question that every person in the world had ever asked and reduced them all to one single question: *why am I?*

This question provided the context that I needed to return to Canada and go to university to study philosophy; and after one year in France I returned to my hometown, worked for a while on the road selling, and then went to university as an adult student to seek an answer to the essential existential question of our existence: *why am I?*

It took many years to come to the realization that this was Noman's question. I eventually came to see that Noman was the *archetypal shadow self* of our personality and essentially non-real insomuch that it was repressed and unconscious; but it was real enough, and finding out that our *shadow self* was real constituted my quest for my true self. In a word, I had to find out why Noman was. I had to find an answer to *"why am I?"*

I left university in my third year because the "mother of all disciplines" had cast me adrift in a sea of endless intellectual speculation, and before I drowned in philosophical doubt I had to get back to *terra firma*; but I did not leave without hope: the divine law of synchronicity determined the next stage of my quest for my true self by way of P. D. Ouspensky's book *In Search of the Miraculous, Fragments of an Unknown Teaching*—the teaching being G. I. Gurdjieff's transformative system of "work on oneself."

In my second year at university I met a student in one of my classes who shared my interests. He hailed from Toronto, and he informed me that he was going home for the Christmas break. I remembered him telling me about his favorite book store, a little New Age book store before the New Age became a movement, and I asked him to bring me back a book that he felt might interest me; and as "chance" would have it, he brought me a book that was exactly what I needed for the next stage of my spiritual quest—though I did not realize this until many years later when I finally put all the pieces together.

Before I fled to France I remember writing in my notebook, "I'm going to go away to look for an answer which I know lies in my own back yard, but I have to go." I did not realize the prophetic implications of this sentiment, but because I became "possessed" one night by an overpowering desire that compelled me to have a sexual experience that shocked my conscience awake I knew that I had to leave; I simply could not continue to live in my hometown where I would be reminded every single day of what I had done. So I sold my business and took an ocean liner from New York City and sailed to Naples, Italy; and from Naples I took a bus to Paris, and then a train to Annecy in the *Aute-Savoie* region of France where life prepared me for the next stage of my spiritual journey.

My sexual experience shocked me, because the person who did what he did that night was me but not me; and I vowed that I would find out who the real me was or die trying. Even though I knew that it was me who was having that sexual experience, I knew in the depths of my soul that it was not me; and this dichotomy of selves catapulted me into my quest for an answer to the deepest question of our being: *who am I?*

I was not consciously aware of it, but after my "big dream" in Annecy (that's what Carl Jung called symbolic dreams that spoke to the collective unconscious) I essentially asked myself the question: **who is the real me: my ego personality, or my soul?** By some miracle of my creative unconscious, *who am I?* and *why am I?* melded into the question *who is the real me?* that addressed the dual nature of the self of man; and I was destined to find the answer. This is why I was condemned to the fourth corner of the abyss in my high school poem "Noman," and why my dream question *why am I?* provided the context that I needed to begin my quest proper for my lost soul by going to university, because I reasoned that it was only logical to begin my search with the "mother of all disciplines."

But when philosophy brought me to the edge of intellectual despair, I was provided once again by the merciful divine law of synchronicity with an opportunity to step upon another path that would help me find an answer to my haunting question that addressed the dual nature of the self of man; and with Gurdjieff's teaching under my arm I stepped out into the cold world to forge my own path to my true self by "creating" my own soul…

7. The Dangers of Kundalini

It's very, very dangerous to awaken the kundalini; it has driven many people out of their mind because they had neither the wisdom nor moral fortitude to tame the "serpent fire." Legend has it that the romantic poets Keats, Shelly, and Byron had all awakened the creative energy of the kundlini with their passion for life; and all three died young.

I have no way of proving this, but I know from experience that the "serpent fire" intensifies one's natural desires to such a degree they can drive one out of his mind, as it did me in my past lifetime as Salaam the Sufi in ancient Persia.

I learned this from one of my past-life regressions, which I included in my novel *Cathedral of My Past Lives* that was inspired by my seven regressions; I failed to pass my initiation into a secret Order of Sufis (how true this is, I have no historical evidence; but it was a very secret Sufi sect called the Order of the White Tiger), and I was banished from the Order when I failed to tame my "tiger of desire."

My "tiger of desire" was the inner beast of all my desires, which had morphed into two distinct desires that I called "the two stallions of my life" that tore me apart—my desire for God, and my desire for sensual pleasure, especially my lust for sex.

To pass my initiation into the secret Order, I had to go out into the world to master my "tiger of desire," and after the allotted time I would meet my Sufi Master in secret for my initiation. It was a test of honor. I was given three opportunities to go out into the world to master my "tiger of desire," but I failed each time; and when I walked out of the house in the dead of night where I was called for my third test, I was a broken man. I was banished from the Order of the White Tiger, and I lost my mind as "the two stallions" of my life tore me apart. I ended up a beggar and died of malnutrition babbling nonsense.

I didn't know it, but my desire for God and my desire for pleasure aroused the "coiled serpent" from its primordial slumber, and

DO WE HAVE AN IMMORTAL SOUL?

I could not control the kundalini energy; that's how I ended up losing myself to the messianic fantasies of my own mind.

I created a fantasy world where I became one with God through the ecstasy of pleasure, and I walked through the towns of ancient Persia spouting verses from the Koran and babbling messianic nonsense; and I was karmically destined to repeat my Sufi life when I accidentally opened up my chakra at the base of my spine and awakened the kundalini while meditating on a maple leaf that night in Annecy, France.

I cannot begin to describe the power that the creative energy of the kundalini had over my mind, and I began to lose myself to a fantasy world of my own making which began innocently enough one evening when my friends invited me to participate in a séance with a Ouija board that unexpectedly opened me up to astral influences; because this experience led to automatic writing, which gave way to such seductive fantasies that had I not experienced going out of my mind in a past life I would have done so again.

I felt beside myself every time I lost myself to my fantasy world, and I knew that no matter how deeply I was pulled into my own mind I could never go insane; because I *knew* that it wasn't me. I simply *knew* that it was another me who wasn't the real me, like a character in a novel of my own creation; but I had to play out my fantasies because the kundalini energy was too powerful to control, and it took the better part of ten years to harness the "serpent fire" and collect myself.

But I would never have been able to do so without Gurdjieff's teaching, which not only gave me the motivation to tame my "tiger of desire," but the means to do so; a system of "work on oneself" that harnessed the wild energies of my awakened kundalini.

That's why I was instantly taken by Ouspensky's book *In Search of the Miraculous, Fragments of an Unknown Teaching,* because I *knew* deep in my soul that Gurdjieff's teaching was precisely the path that I needed to save myself from myself.

Gurdjieff fascinated me so much from the moment I met him in Ouspensky's book that I was pulled into his gravitational field one night in a dream. I dove into his teaching of "work on oneself" the day I left university, and in my dream I asked Gurdjieff if he would accept me into his inner circle of students. He replied that I was not ready yet.

Two years later I met him again in a dream, and he accepted me into his inner circle. I was kneeling in front of him. We were in the center of a large circle of his closest pupils. He placed his hands on my shoulders, and I looked up into his big dark eyes that shone with so much love that it brought tears to my eyes, his bald shiny dome, and his white handlebar moustache; and he said to me in the sweetest voice, "You ready now. I teach you become real man."

Gurdjieff spoke his own peculiar form of English, and he meant that now he could teach me to realize my full potential as a human being. According to Gurdjieff, not everyone is born with an immortal soul; only some people, who due to extraordinary life circumstances managed to create an embryonic soul, and so "man" was only a man in quotation marks until he created his own soul. Only then would he be a real man, and his teaching would do that for me because by "working" on myself with his teaching and my *Royal Dictum* I had managed to create an embryonic soul and could now become a real man. That's why I couldn't stop crying when he accepted me into his inner circle.

I honestly didn't know whether to believe Gurdjieff, because I never really doubted that we are all born with an immoral soul; but I knew in my heart that he was my salvation, so I had no choice but to embrace him as my teacher. I ordered dozens of books on Gurdjieff and his teaching from Samuel Weiser publishers in New York City, and couldn't wait from month to month for my next batch of books to arrive.

Every new book that I read pulled me in deeper into his teaching, and I "worked" on myself with abandoned intensity; especially with my *Royal Dictum*.

My *Royal Dictum* was the bane and salvation of my life. My *Royal Dictum* came to me out of the blue in my second year of philosophy studies. I drove home from Lakehead University one weekend and went for one of my long philosopher's walks through my back yard, down to the CN railroad tracks and to the "Little Black Bridge" all the way to the manmade breakwater that connected the mainland to the little "island" in the middle of the Nipigon River where I sat and smoked half a dozen cigarettes as I pondered my future.

On my way back, I stopped on the breakwater, looked up into the sky, and pleaded from the depths of my anguished soul: *"God, I know that we get nothing for nothing in this world, or any world for that matter, so please tell me; what price truth?"*

Philosophy had brought me to a dead end, and I did not know where to turn; but I was driven by the *daemonic* spirit of my spiritual quest, and I was willing to pay any price to find my true self. And pay, I did...

8. My Royal Dictum

What price truth? It takes a lot of courage to ask this question, and few people ask it for fear of getting an answer; but I had no choice.

I vowed to find my true self or die trying; but the "mother of all disciplines" had brought me to a dead end and I had nowhere to turn but God. I stood on the breakwater in silent despair staring at the Nipigon River as it flowed past me, and as I stared at the river I thought of the Preacher's words in Ecclesiastes: *"All the rivers run into the sea; yet the sea is not full; unto the place from whence the rivers come, thither they return again."*

And then, for no apparent reason I thought of Sophocles' play *Oedipus Rex,* the plague that had befallen his kingdom of Thebes, the edict that Oedipus had decreed banishing whoever was responsible from his kingdom, how the blind prophet Teiresias named King Oedipus himself as the man responsible for killing the former king Laius and marrying his wife Jocasta, who turned out to be Oedipus' father and mother, how his sin of patricide and defilement of his mother's bed were responsible for the blight upon his kingdom, how he gouged his own eyes out and banished himself from his kingdom for his abomination, and suddenly like a bolt of lightning the answer to my question struck me: *"I have to banish myself out of my own kingdom! That's the price I have to pay!"*

In a sudden flash of illumination it came to me that as every river springs from its own source I would have to go to the source of my own life to find my true self, and to do that I had to banish myself out of the kingdom of my own senses; that was the price I had to pay to find my true self, and I took out my pocket notebook and wrote out my *Royal Dictum: "I am like Oedipus Rex. I have exiled myself out of my own kingdom. I embrace my becoming blindly, and I leave all of my sins behind me. I am going to go against the natural course of evolution, and each obstacle that I encounter I will consume."*

DO WE HAVE AN IMMORTAL SOUL?

And from the moment I stepped off the breakwater I threw my cigarettes away and began my journey out of the kingdom of my own senses and pleasures of my life.

So thorough was my insight that I vowed to live my edict of self-denial for the rest of my life, and when I went back into the mainstream of life I was a different man. I flowed against the currents of life now, but I did not share my new discipline with anyone.

I lived my ascetic life of self-denial in secret, which proved to be a Herculean challenge and source of mystery to my family and friends (because I no longer dated, a rumor was started that I was gay); but after three and a half years of living the interior life of self-denial I hit another dead end, and once again the Preacher's words saved me.

I was alone in my separate apartment that I had added onto our family home when for no apparent reason I opened my Bible and read the *Book of Ecclesiastes* in its entirety, and it spoke to me in an entirely new voice; and when I read the last three verses I knew that my *Royal Dictum* had served its purpose and I had to step back into the stream of life.

"And further, by these, my son, be admonished," said the Preacher; *"of making many books there is no end; and much study is a weariness of the flesh. Let us hear the conclusion of the whole matter: Fear God and keep his commandments; for this is the whole duty of man. For God shall bring every work into judgment, with every secret thing, whether it be good, or whether it be evil."*

I put the Bible away and went out. I dropped into the Nipigon Inn Hotel, where I worked part-time as a waiter, and ordered a scotch and water. I spotted Jenny and two other young women and asked if I could join them. We had a few drinks, and I asked Jenny if I could take her home. She said yes. We went to my apartment instead. I put on a cozy fire in my Franklin, and we made love. I was back in the stream of life…

9. When Called, I Had To Go

"To everything there is a season, and a time to every purpose under the heaven," said the Preacher; and I knew that my *Royal Dictum* had served its purpose and I had to jump back into the mainstream of life; but, in all honesty, it was almost as difficult to jump back into life as it was to step out of it.

Only a monk or nun who have taken vows of chastity, poverty, and obedience (I met a former Sister of Mercy who had also taken a vow of service, which inspired my novel *Tea with Grace*) could possibly understand the security that comes with these vows once one has tamed their demons of desire; but be that as it may, I really had no choice, because I *knew* that my *Royal Dictum* had served its purpose and to continue living a life of self-denial would only have hampered my spiritual progress.

Jenny and I dated for a little more than a year, and then she gave me an ultimatum; propose marriage, or she would take a transfer on her job and move away. I could not commit myself, and she accepted the transfer and moved to Southern Ontario.

Two, perhaps three years later she came home for a visit and I took her out for dinner for old time's sake; but she wanted to get back together. I couldn't commit. I was still too caught up in my spiritual quest and it wouldn't have been fair to the relationship.

Once again, we parted company. She found a new man, got married, and gave her children Biblical names; and sadly last year I learned from a post on Facebook that she had died of cancer. Jenny was beautiful and innocent, and I will always remember her fondly; but our life together was not meant to be.

Before I met the woman that I was karmically destined to be with, I dated another woman for seven months. She was ten years older, separated from her alcoholic husband, had a boy in his teens living at home and a married daughter with a young child, and we fell in love; but I could not continue our relationship.

As much as I wanted to, I simply could not. I could see that our relationship would never grow large enough to contain me, and I knew that down the road I would suffer the anguish that forces most relationships to break up; so I decided to end it before the hurt became too much to bear, and I wrote her a letter explaining why we had to part.

I drove to her house in the adjacent community and delivered my letter. She went into the living room, read my letter, waited for what seemed an eternity, and came out with her eyes and nose red from tears. I cried too. But she understood.

"I knew," she said, and told me about her dream. I had given her a golden heart locket and necklace for her birthday, and in her dream she lost it. She woke up and frantically looked in her jewelry box for her locket; but she knew what her dream augured, so my letter didn't come as a total surprise to her. We parted company friends, and I cherish my memories with her. But such was my life; when called, I had to go…

10. Like a Thief in the Night

Was Gurdjieff right? Is man not born with an immoral soul? Gurdjieff called his teaching "esoteric Christianity." Did this mean that Jesus also believed that man is not born with an immortal soul, and that he must be born again to be saved?

"Ye must be born again," said Jesus in the Gospel of John; this is why Gurdjieff called his teaching "esoteric Christianity," because both teachings had to do with this spiritual birth. And there was only one way to give birth to one's spiritual self, which was to "die" to one's life. As the Sufis say, "You must die before you die."

"He that loveth his life shall lose it; and he that hateth his life in this world shall keep it unto life eternal," said Jesus, which I had done with my *Royal Dictum* and Gurdjieff's techniques of *self-remembering, non-identifying, voluntary effort,* and *conscious suffering.*

Gurdjieff's teaching awakened me to the Way; but not entirely without help from a mysterious voice that spoke to me one night. I was sitting alone in my basement bedroom of our family home (this was before I added on a private apartment to our house), wallowing in despair. I had taken Gurdjieff's teaching as far as I could take it, and I came to a disconcerting standstill. I simply could not get any more out of his teaching, despite how much I "worked" on myself with his techniques; and then I heard a voice in my mind.

I don't know if it was a coincidence or not, but I'm pretty sure I heard the voice in my mind as Beethoven's Ode to Joy was playing on my record player, a man's voice that spoke as clear and distinct as if he was standing beside me: *"why do you lie?"*

Startled, I froze. Alert, I turned to look. My bedroom was empty. I listened. Nothing. Just Beethoven's Ninth Symphony. I waited. Still nothing.

"Why do you lie?" I repeated to myself. I couldn't believe it. I tried to make sense of my inexplicable experience. The voice spoke to me in my mind. That's what made it so incredible. It was clearly a

man's voice, and definitely in my own mind; but whose voice was it? And why did it ask me that question?

The question haunted me for days. I couldn't get it out of my mind. *"Why do you lie?"* The more I thought about it, the more it bothered me. I didn't lie. I was a truth seeker. I went out of my way to look for truth. I read hundreds of books looking for truth. I studied philosophy, world religions, psychology, and literature to look for truth; I didn't lie.

But the more I thought about the question, the more I *heard* myself when I talked with people, and I *observed* my actions with my painting customers and everyone I talked to, and I began to see myself in a new light: *I was not entirely honest with people, or with myself.* And thus began the next stage of my journey to my true self…

Ouspensky recorded Gurdjieff's talks in his book, and at one point Gurdjieff said something that didn't hit home with me until I began to see that I wasn't entirely honest with myself: "To speak the truth is the most difficult thing in the world; and one must study a great deal and for a long time in order to be able to speak the truth. The wish alone is not enough. *To speak the truth one must know what the truth is and what a lie is, and first of all in oneself.* But this nobody wants to know" (*In Search of the Miraculous*, p. 22).

This opened up Gurdjieff's teaching of "work on oneself" to me in an entirely new way, because now I had something to work with—*my own false self!* And I went back out into the marketplace with an entirely new purpose—to catch my false self in action and do everything in my power to transform the consciousness of my own falseness!

Now Gurdjieff's teaching began to make sense to me. Now I understood what he meant by our *essence* and *personality*. Our *essence* was our *being* and authentic self, and our *personality* was our *non-being* and inauthentic self; and to become a real man we had to grow in *essence* at the expense of *personality*.

But not only did I have to grow in *essence*; I had to transform what Gurdjieff called my *false personality*. Everyone had one, and the more attention I paid to my thoughts and words and feelings the more I began to see my *false personality*; and it terrified me, because I could not believe how false I really was. *I began to see my unconscious false self!*

Christ's teaching began to make more sense to me, and I began to use his sayings in the same way that I used Gurdjieff's techniques to "work" on myself; and the more I *lived* the sayings of Jesus, the more I woke up to the Way.

"Therefore whosoever heareth these sayings of mine and doeth them, I will liken him unto a wise man, which built his house upon a rock," said Jesus in St. Mathew's Gospel, which was Christ's metaphorical way of saying that one grew in spirit when he put to practice his sayings; and the more I *lived* his sayings, the more I grew in spirit.

But because I also "worked" on myself with Gurdjieff's techniques and lived my *Royal Dictum*, I grew so much in spirit that one evening while waiting on tables at the Nipigon Inn Hotel I experienced such a dramatic shift in consciousness that I can only describe it as breaking out of the prison of my own unconscious falseness.

I had a wicked cold that night, and I *non-identified* with my cold as I waited on customers; and I made monumental efforts to *non-identify* with the strippers as they gyrated their seductively naked bodies on stage, and I actually experienced a "snap" inside me as I shifted my center of gravity from my inauthentic to authentic self— *and from that moment on I could tell a lie from the truth in myself, and this changed my life forever!*

My experience at the Nipigon Inn Hotel was one of the most memorable experiences in my entire life, because I actually felt a "snap" inside me as I sprung free from the unconsciousness prison of my false self. I cannot describe how free I felt.

This experience took me a long time to understand, but it was not without precedent in the Gurdjieff Work. The literary critic and editor of the influential journal *The New Age* in London, England before selling it in 1922 and moving to Fontainebleau, France to study under Gurdjieff, A. R. Orage had a similar experience, and he actually used the same word "snap" to describe what he experienced when he had a sudden shift in consciousness after making an enormous effort of will to do what Gurdjieff had asked him to do.

DO WE HAVE AN IMMORTAL SOUL?

Orage was an intellectual who edited and published such brilliant writers as George Bernard Shaw, H. G. Wells, T. S. Elliot, Ezra Pound, and the very talented and promising New Zealand short story writer Katherine Mansfield in his *The New Age* weekly; so when Gurdjieff told him to dig a trench at the Priory and then fill it back up again for no apparent reason other than to just dig and fill it back up, his formidable intellect was nonplussed, but he continued to dig because Gurdjieff must have had his reasons.

And he dug and *non-identified* with his digging. He dug and *non-identified* and dug and *non-identified* and dug and *non-identified*, and after days of relentless digging and *non-identifying* he felt a "snap" and was released from himself.

That's what happened to me. I waited on tables and *non-identified* with my cold and naked strippers (remember, I had awakened the kundalini and had ENORMOUS sexual sensitivity), and worked and *non-identified*, and worked and *non-identified* until I felt a "snap" and liberated myself from my unconscious self; and I was FREE.

Orage experienced the same inner freedom when he experienced that "snap," but the difference between Orage and me was that I had liberated myself from the prison of my unconscious falseness and Orage had liberated himself from the prison of his intellect; and from that moment on he *understood* the Work because it made sense to him now, which is why he went on to describe Gurdjieff's Work as "sublime common sense." He finally saw the metabiological benefit of the teaching, and devoted the rest of his life to the Work.

According to Gurdjieff, man was asleep; and the purpose of the Work was to wake man up. When I experienced that "snap" I woke up to myself, because I had broken the unconscious hold that my false self had upon me; and Orage broke the unconscious hold that his intellect had upon him. With enormous effort of will, Orage and I created enough consciousness by *non-identifying* with what we were doing to "snap" the hold that our unconscious self had over us; not unlike filling a balloon with air until it bursts.

And I began to grow in *essence* like never before, because now that I had become conscious of my false self it had no more power over me. I was so conscious of myself that I could no longer

29

tell an unconscious lie—*not to mention how painful it was when I told a conscious lie!*—and it was so much easier to store my treasures in heaven now, as Jesus expressed the secret teaching of the Way:

> *"Lay not up for yourselves treasures upon earth, where moth and rust doth corrupt, and where thieves break through and steal. But lay up for yourselves treasures in heaven, where neither moth nor rust doth corrupt, and where thieves do not break through nor steal. For where your treasure is, there will your heart be also. The light of the body is the eye; if therefore thine eye be single, thy whole body shall be full of light. But if thine eye be evil, thy whole body is full of darkness. If therefore the light that is in thee be darkness, how great is that darkness! No man can serve two masters; for either he will hate the one, and love the other; or else he will hold the one, and despise the other. Ye cannot serve God and mammon,"* said Jesus in the Gospel of Mathew (6: 19-24).

Gurdjieff's simple technique of *non-identifying* with whatever one does was next to impossible to master, but the more effort I made to *non-identify* with the object of my concern, the more effective I became in the metabiological alchemy of *non-identifying*.

The best way to describe the technique of *non-identifying* would be *doing without doing,* an active form of non-attachment; which I came to realize was the paradoxical center of Christ's teaching of spiritual rebirth. And the more I "worked" on myself with Gurdjieff's teaching, the more Christ's paradoxical sayings made sense to me; until one day I simply woke up to the omniscient guiding force of life. And many years later I wrote my novel *Jesus Wears Dockers, The Gospel Conspiracy Story* (and the sequel, *St. Paul's Conceit*) to explain the secret teaching of the Way encoded in Christ's sayings.

The Way is always there to assist us in our journey through life; and the more conscious I became of the Way, the more I saw the Way in my everyday life—in my conversations with people, on a television program, a book or magazine that I was reading, or whatever; the Way was the silent voice of God that spoke to me like messages of highlighted wisdom, and I listened, learned, and lived the *Golden-tongued messages* of the Way with passionate intensity until I stored enough treasures in heaven that one fine summer day I unexpectedly gave birth to my spiritual self in my mother's kitchen while she was kneading bread dough on the kitchen table!

It stole upon me like a thief in the night, just as Jesus said it would. One moment everything was normal as I talked with my mother, and the next moment I'm overtaken by a feeling of absolute certainty that I was immortal and would never die. *In the twinkle of an eye, my whole life changed; and I have never doubted my immortal self since.*

11. Waking Up to Life

Gurdjieff was WRONG. In February, 1923 Professor Denis Saurat, director of the French Institute in London, visited his friend and literary critic A. R. Orage at the Priory in Fontainebleau-Avon, France to see what Gurdjieff's Institute for the Harmonious Development of Man was all about (rumor had it that strange things went on there); and he interviewed the enigmatic man whose teaching had the power to induce Orage to sell his highly respected weekly journal and go to France to study the Work.

Professor Saurat asked Gurdjieff if man had an immoral soul, and Gurdjieff replied: *"Few human beings have a soul. Nobody has a soul at birth. One must acquire a soul. Those who do not succeed in this die. The atoms disperse and nothing remains (after death). Some make a partial soul and are then subject to a kind of reincarnation that permits them to progress. Finally, a very small number of men succeed in possessing immortal souls."*

Nature will only evolve us so far and no further, said Gurdjieff; and to continue evolving we have to take evolution into our own hands. That's what his teaching was all about, and why he attracted so many intelligent people to the Work; especially creative writers, who have a highly developed intuitive relationship with life.

I'm a writer, and I know how the creative process works. To quote Adrienne Rich, *"poetry* (creative writing) *is an act of the imagination that transforms reality into a deeper perception of what is."* Which makes writers truth seekers despite themselves.

Writers seek to understand life and make sense of the human condition; this is why writers are looked upon as the natural prophets of our society. As Shelly said in his iconic essay *In the Defense of Poetry*, "poets are the unacknowledged legislators of the world."

But the creative process can only take one so far, and no further; this is why so many artists were, and still are attracted to the Gurdjieff Work. To finish what nature left unfinished, one has to find the Way; the path to "wholeness and singleness of self," as Carl Jung expressed the ultimate purpose of the individuation process.

DO WE HAVE AN IMMORTAL SOUL?

This was Gurdjieff's promise, and my attraction to his teaching. But after I gave birth to my spiritual self I had to move on, because the Work no longer satisfied my new spiritual needs. And once again, the merciful law of synchronicity introduced me to my new path by way of a distant cousin who dropped by our house to visit my mother one summer day.

By pure chance, which I now attribute to providential design, I just happened to come home from work just as my cousin was visiting my mother. She was standing at the kitchen sink filling a blue plastic container with tap water to take to her cottage; but she had a doctor's appointment and couldn't stay very long.

"Do you believe in reincarnation?" she asked me, out of the blue. My cousin was known to be flighty and off-the-wall. She had a very idiosyncratic personality.

"Yes, of course," I replied.

"Then you might be interested in a new teaching I discovered. It's based on karma and reincarnation. You know what karma is, don't you?"

"Yes," I said, smiling. "You can't have reincarnation without karma."

"Why don't you drop by the cottage later? I have some books you can borrow."

"Maybe I will," I said, to humor her; but I had no intention of driving out to her cottage because my ego could not relish the idea of being introduced to a new path by a flakey cousin with her gypsy ways, but that evening on my way to the restaurant for a cup of coffee I could not deny the nudge that compelled me to explore this new path.

She showed me half a dozen books, but I selected one which I began to devour the moment I got home; and when I got to chapter two and read the following words, I knew I had found my new spiritual path; **or, rather, it had found me, proving yet again that when the student is ready, the teacher appears:**

"The way is neither to the right, nor to the left. It is not below you or above you but it is here; the way to enter into the Far Country. Christ said that the way into the Kingdom of Heaven, meaning the Far Country, was within. But he was wrong. He said again in the

Gospel of John that He was the Way, as the Christ. And again I say that he was wrong! Now I tell you, the way into Heaven IS! That is what I can tell you in so many words—this and this alone, for it is the same as saying that God IS!"

For personal reasons, I choose not to mention the name of the book where this came from, nor the author; but the moment I read those words I exclaimed, "I'M HOME!"

I had awakened to the Way by "working" on myself with absolute resolve, and those words resonated so deeply with every fiber of my being that I had no choice but to embrace this new spiritual path, generically known to the world as The Way of the Eternal; and to this day, more than thirty years later, I still embrace the spiritual principles of this path—*despite the fact that I have also outgrown it!*

If I may, The Way of the Eternal is both an inner and outer path. I have outgrown the *outer teachings* of this path, which is now a structured organized New Age religion centered in the United States and established in countries throughout the world; but I continue to be guided by the *inner teachings* of this path, which come to me by way of my Inner Guide (my Higher Self), dreams, insights, nudges, signs, symbols, coincidences, and especially synchronicities. In a word, I live the Way *consciously* today.

In their book *Spiritual Literacy, Reading the Sacred in Everyday Life,* husband and wife team Frederic and Mary Ann Brussat quote John Shea, a contemporary Catholic theologian, who has come closer than anyone that I have read to explaining what is meant by the astonishing statement "The Way just IS!" John Shea says:

"The spiritual life is, at root, a matter of seeing. It is all of life seen from a certain perspective. It is waking, sleeping, dreaming, eating, drinking, working, loving, relaxing, recreating, walking, sitting, standing, and breathing...spirit suffuses everything; and so ***the spiritual life is simply life***, wherever and whatever, seen from the vantage point of spirit" (*Spiritual Literacy*, p. 28; bold italics mine).

DO WE HAVE AN IMMORTAL SOUL?

This is just another way of saying that the Way *is* life; but to realize this one has to wake up to how life works. That's what Gurdjieff's teaching helped me do, because as I "worked" on myself with his techniques I expanded my consciousness and woke up to my unconscious self and the life process until one day I woke up to the omniscient guiding force of life; that's how I gravitated to Christ's secret teaching of the Way.

12. Love, Mercy, and Compassion

"Many are called but few are chosen," said Jesus; which implies that one has to be ready for the secret teachings of the Way that he brought to the world.

When Jesus was asked by the cynical lawyer what he had to do for eternal life, Jesus gave him the Parable of the Good Samaritan. This is the best known of all of Christ's parables, because it contains the essential message of his teaching. I explored this parable in my little book *Why Bother? The Riddle of the Good Samaritan,* which explains what Jesus meant by his mystifying comment "many are called but few are chosen."

The priest who walked by the injured man by the side of the road was not ready for the kingdom of heaven; that's why he did not stop to help him. And the Levite who walked by the injured man did not stop to help him either, because he also was not ready for the kingdom of heaven; but the Samaritan who stopped to help the injured man was ready for the kingdom of heaven, because he had something that the priest and Levite did not have.

The injured man by the side of the road "called" the priest and Levite to help him, but they did not hear his silent call for help and were not chosen to enter the kingdom of heaven; they had to be "cooked" some more by life to be made ready for the Way, as the Sufis say. But the Samaritan heard the silent call and helped the injured man and was chosen for the kingdom of heaven; that's why Jesus told the cynical lawyer to go out and do as the Good Samaritan and he would have eternal life in the kingdom of heaven.

It was not in the priest's character, nor the Levite's to show mercy on the injured man; but the Samaritan not only nursed the injured man's wounds, but put him on his beast of burden and brought him to an inn and paid the innkeeper to look after him until he returned from his trip to Jericho.

The Samaritan had compassion for the injured man, but not the priest and Levite; so the silent call that they did not hear was *the call of compassion* for their fellow man, it was *the call of mercy* for their fellow man, and it was *the call of love* for their fellow man; and that's the moral of the Good Samaritan.

Love, mercy, and compassion for our fellow man; that's why Jesus died on the cross for the world: he sacrificed his life to show us the Way. *"He who has ears to hear, let him hear,"* said Jesus…

.

13. The Buddhist Fallacy

I was born to become a seeker. At the risk of revealing something about myself that may put whatever I have to say about the immortal soul of man in an entirely new light, one which may not shine favorably upon me, I have to reveal something that I learned about myself during one of my spiritual healing sessions with a gifted psychic medium.

Three years ago the variables of my life miraculously converged to give rise to another life-changing synchronicity: I attended an open house for Angie's new storefront practice in the business section of the city (Angie is the fictional name that I gave to the psychic medium in my novel *Healing with Padre Pio*); and she gave me a complimentary spiritual healing and I learned that St. Padre Pio was one of her spiritual guides.

Padre Pio is a Roman Catholic Saint. He is known throughout the Christian world as the healing saint who suffered the holy wounds of Jesus most of his life. He had visitations from Jesus and the Holy Mother, and he was born in a poor region of Italy not far from where I was born; so when Angie told me that he was one of her spiritual guides my curiosity about spiritual healing instantly gave birth to the idea for my next novel.

I had ten spiritual healing sessions with St. Padre Pio, whom Angie channeled with astonishing clarity; and in my ninth or tenth session he told me something about myself that took me completely by surprise: *he told me that I have lived my same life over again three different times, and my current life is one of those times!*

This is how I was introduced to the concept of parallel lives, which completely shifted my paradigm on reincarnation. But he also introduced me to a book that would shed light upon this new paradigm: *Love without End, Jesus Speaks*, by the portrait artist Glenda Green; the true story of Glenda's experience with Jesus, how he manifested in her studio so she could paint his portrait ("The Lamb and The Lion"), and also reveal to her that part of his secret teaching that he could not reveal to the public during his ministry because it was not given to the public to know the mysteries of the kingdom of heaven:

"And the disciples came, and said unto him, Why speakest thou unto them in parables? He answered and said unto them, Because it is given unto you to know the mysteries of the kingdom of heaven, but to them it is not given. For whosoever hath, to him shall be given, and he shall have more abundance; but whosoever hath not, from him shall be taken away even that he hath. Therefore speak I to them in parables: because they seeing see not; and hearing they hear not, neither do they understand" (Math. 13: 10-13).

It never occurred to me before that reincarnation was anything more than a linear progression from one life to the next, each life largely pre-destined by our former life for the specific purpose of evolving in consciousness until we are mature enough to take karmic responsibility for our own life and break the cycle of life and death; but now that I had been introduced to the concept of parallel lives my spiritual horizons began to expand.

"Life is all about growth and understanding," St. Padre Pio told me in one of my sessions, and obviously I was ready to have my personal paradigm expanded; that's why he informed me that I chose to be reborn into my same life again so that I could change the outcome of my life. Apparently the first time that I lived my life as Orest Stocco I was close-minded about "that other religion" (my current spiritual path), but this time I'm not—obviously, since I've been living it for the past thirty years!

It blew my mind to learn that I'm living my same life over again to change the outcome of my life; but it does explain a strange dream I had many years ago.

I dreamt that I was in my senior years walking up to the post office in my hometown of Nipigon, and as I walked to get my mail I felt enormous regret for not having lived the life I felt I should have lived. I felt empty and unfulfilled, like I had betrayed myself; and I went to my grave a very sad and disappointed man. That's why I returned to live my same life over again; ***I had to reclaim my lost opportunity to find my lost soul!***

After I wrote *Healing with Padre Pio* I dove into my research on parallel lives, and it didn't take long to learn that parallel worlds have become a preoccupation of quantum physics; which inspired the idea for a new book on my parallel life.

I loved the challenge of writing about my parallel life, but I had no idea how to go about it; and then it occurred to me to start with my dreams, because "dreams are messages of the soul" (Carl Jung), and soul exists in the Eternal Now; ergo, dreams speak to all of our lives—past, present, future, and parallel lives.

In *Edgar Cayce on Dreams*, by Harmon H. Bro, Ph.D., ("Under the editorship of Hugh Lynn Cayce"), Cayce said: **"They (dreams) work to accomplish two things. They work to solve the problems of the dreamer's conscious, waking life. And they work to quicken in the dreamer new potentials which are his to claim."**

The "problem" of my conscious waking life was to understand why I was living my same life over again, so I felt it only prudent to start another dream journal; which I did, and soon my dreams began sending me messages that helped me solve my problem and quicken my new potentials which were mine to claim—one new potential being my new book *The Summoning of Noman, The True Story of My Parallel Life.*

I *knew* I had lived past lives because I had at least four past-life recollection dreams in my youth and seven past-life regressions eight years ago, which helped me to understand my current life (why Penny and I had to meet to work out our past-life karma, for example); and I also knew that we can have future-life recollections dreams, because I had one.

In my future-life dream I'm a very precocious young writer. I'm born with a natural talent for creative writing, and I'm obsessed with words. I study words from the earliest age, because I have an instinctual knowledge that words are windows on man's soul; so I devour words like other children devour candy. And I'm constantly writing.

I did not know that this was a future-life recollection dream until synchronicity introduced me to Dr. Bruce Goldberg's book *Past Lives, Future Lives Revealed* and learned that under hypnosis one can be "progressed" to a future lifetime. I wasn't hypnotized, but I did dream of my future life as a very gifted young writer. But this did not shock me, really; because it's only logical that all of my efforts to become a writer in my current lifetime would karmically bear fruit in a future life; and I started my new dream journal because I wanted to come to terms with my parallel life. That's what I sought to explore with my new book *The Summoning of Noman, The True Story of My Parallel Life.*

So it was very comforting to have my new perspective on reincarnation confirmed and expanded upon even further by none other than Jesus himself. Glenda Green writes:

"Eventually, I had the courage to use the word 'reincarnation.' 'What do you have to say about the subject of past and future lives?'

"His reply was to the point. *'Your immortality is a simple thing, and so your understanding will be more accurate if you keep it simple as well. By the will of God, life creates a place for you infinitely again and again, according to your love and in relation to your loved ones.'*

"He cautioned, *'The philosophy of reincarnation is not that simple. It does affirm your continuity, and that is good. However, there's a twist in it which defers your immortality back to structure and linearity, which is not true. Your immortality is not imprisoned within a wheel of life, or pathways of cause and effect. Neither are you the product of linear evolvement. You were created in perfection, and perfect love, and you do **continue** to re-manifest infinitely, but it is according to the will of the Father and according to your own purposes, your own love, and your own place of service and learning.'* He added, with a touch of humor, *'You actually only have one life! It's just a very long one, with many chapters"* (Love without End, Jesus Speaks pp. 76-7).

WOW! I couldn't have asked for a better explanation for the secret doctrine of reincarnation. In one fell swoop Jesus appears to bridge the great divide that I felt existed between the Buddhist perspective on reincarnation (which does not believe in the individual soul) and the perspective that the individual soul reincarnates from one life to the next; according to how we interpret Jesus then, both views are correct.

OREST STOCCO

But how can this be? How can Buddhists, who don't believe we have an autonomous self, be correct when Jesus clearly says that we do continue to re-manifest infinitely in accordance to the will of the Father and *according to our own purposes, our own love, and according to our own place of service and learning?*

Jesus clearly implies our own individual karmic destiny with his reference to **"our own purpose," "our own love,"** and **"our own place of service and learning,"** just as I had worked it out with my own past-life regressions; but according to Jesus we also only live one very long life with many chapters, which could imply the Buddhist perspective.

What reincarnates according to Buddhism is not an autonomous self, but the stream of infinite *I Am* consciousness that re-manifests in another body—*one very long life with many chapters!* As Tibetan monk Matthieu Ricard explains to his father Jean-Francois Revel in their book *The Monk and the Philosopher,* "Buddhism accepts that there is a continuum of consciousness, but denies any existence of a solid, permanent, and autonomous self anywhere in that continuum. The essence of Buddhist practice is therefore to get rid of that illusion of a self which so falsifies our view of the world." And he goes on to say, to further affirm the Buddhist perspective, "That the self has no true existence doesn't prevent one particular stream of consciousness from having qualities that distinguish it from another stream" (pp. 35 and 34 respectively).

This is the *Buddhist fallacy,* which offends me to the core; and at the risk of showing my cards before I'm called upon to play my hand, I have personal proof in one of my past-life regressions that the Buddhist perspective on the self of man is a misperception of Soul's natural impulse to individuate the consciousness of God; but that will have to wait...

14. Literature Is Not Enough

"Prior to everything, I already am," wrote Andrew Cohen in his book *Evolutionary Enlightenment, A New Path to Spiritual Awakening.* And he goes on to say, "The experience of this recognition is not one of *becoming* liberated. It is of being *already* liberated."

Again, I don't disagree with this perspective; what I disagree with is the idea that we can put the carriage in front of the horse, because if we *already* are liberated then what is the purpose of life? Why evolution? Why the whole process of *becoming*? Why would the acorn seed want to *become* an oak tree when it *already* is an oak tree?

This is the *Buddhist fallacy* that defies the logic of life, because every person in the world has a natural impulse to realize "wholeness and singleness of self." Katherine Mansfield, whose tragic young life speaks to the very process of *becoming* one's true self, addressed the *Buddhist fallacy* as well as any person's life can, because her path of creative writing brought her as far as it possibly could to her true self; that's why despite her doctor's strong objections she went to the Priory in Fontainebleau to meet Gurdjieff and study his teaching to reconnect with the self that she had lost.

Katherine Mansfield was dying of tuberculosis, and the confrontation with her mortality set her soul ablaze with the desire to save herself. In a letter written from the Priory to her husband, the writer John Middleton Murry, dated October 18, 1922 she wrote: "…in the deepest sense I've always been disunited. And this which has been my 'secret sorrow' for years has become everything to me just now. I really can't go on pretending to be one person and being another anymore, Boge. It is a living death. So, I have decided to make a clean sweep of all that was 'superficial' in my past life and start again to see if I can get into that real living, simple, truthful, *full* life I dream of. I have been through a horrible deadly time coming to this. You know the kind of time. It doesn't show much, outwardly, but one is simply chaos within!" (*Gurdjieff,* Chapter 12: "Katherine Mansfield's Last Hope," by Louis Pauwells, pp.208-9).

Orage was living at the Priory at the time and they had many long talks about writing and the Work before she died at the age of 34. Orage wrote in the little book *A. R. Orage ON LOVE, With Some Aphorisms & Other Essays*: "The real reason, and only reason, that led Katherine Mansfield to the Gurdjieff Institute was less dissatisfaction with her craftsmanship than dissatisfaction with herself; less dissatisfaction with her stories than with the attitude toward life implied in them; less dissatisfaction with her own and contemporary literature than with literature…'Suppose', she used to say, 'that I could succeed in writing as well as Shakespeare. It would be lovely, but what then? There is something wanting in literary art even at its highest. Literature is not enough" (p. 38).

Katherine made the great discovery that all creative writers will make one day, that "major literature is an initiation into truth." *But where does one go after he comes to this realization?* "Where is the writer with the keys of initiation upon him?" asks Orage. "This was Katherine Mansfield introduction to the Gurdjieff institute, and the object of her travel there," says Orage—BECAUSE SHE WAS READY FOR THE SECRET TEACHINGS OF THE WAY; just as Orage was ready, which was why he sold his *New Age* journal and went to the Priory to become a student of Gurdjieff's teaching.

To the outside world the Gurdjieff Institute was a suspicious place, but Katherine's husband wrote: "It is not for me to pass judgment on the Gurdjieff Institute. I cannot tell whether Katherine's life was shortened by her entry into it. But I am persuaded of this: that Katherine made of it an instrument for that process of self-annihilation which is necessary to the spiritual rebirth, whereby we enter the Kingdom of Heaven. I am certain that she achieved her purpose, and that the Institute lent itself to it. More I dare not, and less I must not, say" (*Gurdjieff*, by Louis Pauwels, p. 312).

Katherine went to Gurdjieff because she saw in his teaching a way to authenticate her life. She wrote in her journal: "Katherine Mansfield. She has led, ever since she can remember, a very typically false life. Yet, through it all, there have been moments, instant gleams, when she felt the possibility of something quite other" (Ibid., p. 251).

This *"something quite other"* was what she sought. She *knew* deep in her soul that there was something false about her life; that's why in an earlier conversation with Orage some months before she went to the Priory she told him that she could not read any of the stories she had written without feeling self-contempt. "There is not one," she said, "that I dare show to God." Why? What did her stories lack that she could not show them to God?

Ernest Hemingway called Katherine Mansfield's stories "near beer." That's a very harsh thing to say about a gifted young writer's stories; but near beer is not the real thing, which was Hemingway's way of saying that they lacked ontological gravitas—i. e., they were more imaginative than real, and therefore near beer.

When I was living in France I dreamt of Hemingway one night, and he gave me a piece of advice about writing that I will never forget. I was offended by what he said, and it took a few years to appreciate his rude comment; but to make his point, which is the same point that he made about Katherine Mansfield's stories, he said to me: "I have pissed out more life than you have lived." In other words, I had to live life before I could write about it truly, because that's the difference between **real** and **near beer**; which is why F. Scott Fitzgerald lauded the young Hemingway as "the real thing" when he recommended him to his now-legendary editor Maxwell Perkins at *Scribner's.*

Ernest Hemingway, a "man's man," lived his life with passionate intensity and wrote about it. He loved to fish, hunt, drink, box, and make love (he had four wives); but his true love was always writing. He lived to write, and he wrote about life as he experienced it. In *A Moveable Feast,* the melancholy memoir that he wrote at the end of his Hemingway-weary life before ending it in Ketchum, Idaho with one of his shotguns, he recalls his lonely apprenticeship days in Paris, how he dreaded not being able to write, and to lift his own spirits he counseled himself with what has become iconic advice to neophyte writers:

"I would stand and look out over the roofs of Paris and think, 'Do not worry. You have always written before and you will write now. *All you have to do is write one true sentence. Write the truest sentence that you know.* So finally I would write one true sentence and go on from there.*" (A Moveable Feast*, p. 12, italics mine)

45

When he was interviewed by George Plimpton for *The Paris Review* in the spring of 1958, Hemingway said: "The most essential gift for a good writer is a built-in, shockproof, shit detector. This is the writer's radar, and all great writers have had it."

All great writers want to get to the truth of life, and they do; that's what makes their work great literature; to wit, Hemingway's *The Old Man and the Sea.* But as Katherine Mansfield realized, literature is not enough. There had to be a way to satisfy that longing in her soul that literature could not satisfy; that's why she was pulled to the Gurdjieff Institute at the Priory where she lived for a few more months before she died.

"I give you good leather, but you must make own shoes," said Gurdjieff to his students at the Priory. In other words, Gurdjieff provided a "key" to the mysteries of life, but they had to initiate themselves. This is why he never tired of telling his students that there was only self-initiation into the mysteries of life, which Orage realized in one euphoric moment when he was digging that cursed trench at the Priory.

Orage realized inner freedom when he experienced the inner "snap" that liberated him from the unconscious hold his intellect had upon him, and I also realized inner freedom when I experienced the inner "snap" that night at the Nipigon Inn Hotel; and that's what Katherine Mansfield wanted from Gurdjieff's teaching that literature could not provide: *she wanted the key that would set her free from herself!*

15. Driven By My Daemon

The more I lived the Way, the more the Way revealed itself to me; that's how I initiated myself into the mysteries of life. And by Way I mean Gurdjieff's system of "work on oneself," my *Royal Dictum,* Christ's sayings, as well as all the little gems of *Golden-tongued wisdom* that I garnered from life. I walked my talk, as it were.

After I had my seven past-life regressions my *daemon* drove me to write with a passion I had never experienced before (half a dozen books in two years while still working my physically exhausting trade of drywall taping and painting), and I began to connect the dots very quickly; and soon I caught a glimpse of the Divine Plan of God, and something that had been puzzling me for years finally began to make sense to me.

Nature can only evolve man so far and no further, said Gurdjieff; and as I came to learn through my studies of Jung, the ancient Alchemists also held this same belief. That's what their teaching was all about; to complete what nature left unfinished. But why can't nature complete what it started? Why do we have to take evolution into our own hands to realize our inherent potential as human beings?

According to Gurdjieff, man is not born with an immortal soul; only the potential to create his own soul. This is a hard truth. So hard that it cast a terrifying pall over the whole Gurdjieff movement; that's why his teaching can drive one to the edge of despair, and right over the edge as Louis Pauwels tells us in his book *Gurdjieff.*

But after I had my seven past-life regressions I saw the *Gurdjieff fallacy,* and a great wave of compassion washed over me for everyone who took Gurdjieff to heart. **He was wrong**. We are all born with an immortal soul, and I will show my cards when I'm called upon to play my hand; but that does not mean that Gurdjieff's teaching was misleading. On the contrary, Gurdjieff's teaching works; just not as he said it would, that's all.

We can't create what we already are, but we can transform the consciousness of what we are with his teaching and realize our Soul self. That's the impenetrable mystery of the Way; but I broke the code, so I know how the Way works. And that's how I came to solve the riddle of why we have to complete what nature left unfinished.

Being and non-being. I wish I could recall my reference, but I've read so many books in my quest for my true self that sometimes it's impossible to recall the exact book for my reference; nonetheless, it was comforting to have my perspective on the natural process of individuation verified by a source other than my own experience.

I know it was a Sufi Master who verified my experience, but he said that there are essentially two paths in life: one path is by way of our *being*; and the other is by way of our *non-being;* and depending upon which path we are on determines our individual way to "wholeness and singleness of self." But what does this mean?

A number of years ago, before I had my seven past-life regressions, I had another one of those strange teaching dreams that took me years to understand; I dreamt of two Hollywood movie directors who represented the two paths in life. One director represented the way of *being*, and the other the way of *non-being*.

I had absolutely no idea what this dream meant at the time. I had to connect a lot of dots before I could see the full picture of the natural process of individuation, and what I saw gave me an insight into human nature that went a long way to solving the mystery of the self of man: I saw the dual nature of the self in the character of the two directors.

Both directors were very successful, with an impressive list of movies to their credit; but they were very different kinds of directors. One was kind, generous, understanding, and very patient with his actors and cast members; and the other was quick-tempered, unforgiving, and so demanding that he made life hell for everyone on his set. He was the exact opposite of the other director. And yet, they were friends. Not personally, of course; but professionally they respected each other and shared views over a drink or two.

In my dream I saw that the director who was kind, generous, and understanding was not uncomfortable with his life. All in all, he had lived a good life; and despite all of his ups and downs he managed to resolve his major conflicts and continue his journey to "wholeness and singleness of self" by taking an interest in spiritual literature. His personal path of directing movies had made him ready for the Way, and despite himself he became a seeker; that's how he spent his private time. Publically, he gave back to his profession by establishing a school *a la* Norman Jewison on the art of making movies.

Despite his very successful career, the other director was a conflicted man. He was unconscionably selfish and miserable with everyone, and he was more miserable alone and sought the company of women, the younger the better. This life was all there was for him, and he drank, smoked, and swore foul obscenities. He was not a happy camper. And he had no desire to give anything back to his profession, which had cost him his soul.

That was my dream, which made no sense to me until I connected the dots and realized that the happy director had taken the way of *being*, and the miserable director had taken the way of *non-being*; because in my own quest for my true self I came to the realization that as long as one remains trapped by the consciousness of their *non-being* they can never, ever be happy; but why? That's the existential mystery of *being* and *non-being* and why the natural process of life cannot evolve us any further...

At university I became fascinated by the philosophers Jean Paul Sartre and Albert Camus. Both were creative writers, and both were awarded the Nobel Prize for literature; the younger Camus first, and then Sartre. But Sartre declined the prize because he felt that he would lose his independence if he accepted. "If I sign my name Jean Paul Sartre, Nobel Prize recipient, it will not be the same as signing my name Jean Paul Sartre," he explained, which spoke to his philosophy of personal freedom.

"Man is condemned to be free," said Sartre, which opened the floodgates to his philosophy of existentialism that washed over society after the Second World War; but because Sartre was an atheist, his philosophy trapped man in the dynamic consciousness of *being* and *becoming*—hence his great work *Being and Nothingness.*

Being and Nothingness is a very long and turgid essay in phenomenological ontology, which essentially was Sartre's study of the consciousness of *being*; and he concludes his philosophy with the realization, "I am what I am not, and I am not what I am."

Because he did not believe in God and the spiritual life, Sartre condemned man to the eternal existential dynamic of *being* and *becoming*; but he was free to choose what he would be within this dynamic, which gave birth to a whole philosophy of *good* and *bad faith*.

In the process of *becoming*, man is not what he is and is what he is not; he is a paradox of *being* and *non-being*. And because Sartre saw no purpose beyond the existential reality of *being* and *becoming*, he concluded that "life is a useless passion."

Camus also concluded that life was essentially absurd, and he created a whole philosophy on the absurdity of life. "One must imagine Sisyphus happy," he sums up in his famous essay *"The Myth of Sisyphus,"* trying desperately to put a brave face on our miserable fate; but I could never imagine myself happy rolling a rock up a hill for eternity.

The fate of Sisyphus was Camus' metaphor for the drudgery of our daily life, but there had to be a way out of this existential dynamic of *being* and *becoming*; and after I extracted all the goodness that I could from their despairing philosophies, I thanked them for their insights into the ontological nature of man and moved on to another path which, as I said, came to me by way of Ouspensky's book *In Search of the Miraculous, Fragments of an Unknown Teaching* that introduced me to Gurdjieff's teaching of the Work.

And I "worked" on myself with such pathological commitment that I transcended myself when I gave birth to my spiritual self in my mother's kitchen that fine summer day while she was kneading bread dough on the kitchen table; and with a song in my heart I wrote in my journal: *"I am what I am not, and I am not what I am; I am both, but neither: I am Soul,"* thereby resolving the paradoxical nature of the *being* and *non-being* aspects of my contingent mortal life and opened the door to the next stage of my spiritual journey…

16. Life Is Merely Something That I Do

Little did I know what I had done, but by "working" on myself I managed to resolve the paradoxical consciousness of my *being* and *non-being*. In Christ's words, I made the two into one; and my new non-paradoxical state of consciousness was my realized Soul self, but it took quite a few years to understand that I had "squared the circle."

I had given birth to my spiritual self, but I did not know it; all I knew was that I *was* immortal, and nothing could take that away from me. The acorn seed had *become* the oak tree, as it were; and from that moment on it was no longer a question of *becoming*, but one of *being*—because I had finally *become* my true self!

I had made one self out of the dual consciousness of my *being* and *non-being*. My new state of consciousness was pure enough for my individuating Soul self to become aware of its immortal nature, and I *coincided* with myself. Which is what Jesus meant by the outer becoming like the inner and the male with the female neither male nor female.

To my delight, I reflected my new state of consciousness in a poem that I wrote a few years after I gave birth to my spiritual self. I was so moved by Penny's mother's death that I had to give expression to my emotions, and I wrote the following poem:

I Am

I felt ashamed of life when I saw her frail body
fighting for its life in the Emergency Room,
emaciated, and heaving like a bellows for air;
I saw no dignity in the physical struggle
to stay alive, no grace, no love, no honor,
just a bodily organism in the throes of death.
I walked home alone from the hospital,
the lonely moon as big as the Eye of God
and the stars sparkling like lost souls in heaven,

and I thought of life and death and everything
in between, and in my heart I smiled for all
of my efforts, struggles, and humiliations to find
my true self, because as I spied death steal
my lover's mother's life I knew, I simply knew,
that I am and life is merely something that I do.

With my spiritual rebirth I shifted my center of gravity (my I-consciousness) from my outer self (my ego-personality) to my inner Soul self; but this did not confer upon me instant spiritual enlightenment that one would expect with spiritual rebirth. Not at all. I had just finished what nature could not do; that's all. From that moment on it was no longer a question of *becoming* my true self, but of simply *being* my true self. My life was the same as before, only my center of gravity had shifted from my outer to inner self.

But I foresaw my spiritual rebirth years before it happened. I was in my second year at university, shortly after I found Gurdjieff's teaching. I was living with three other adult students in a house that we had rented for the term, and I was in my bedroom one night trying to make sense of Gurdjieff's teaching; but I just didn't get it.

I read *In Search of the Miraculous* and Gurdjieff's teaching spoke to me, but I couldn't grasp the message; and this frustrated me so much that I threw the book down in disgust and shut the lights out and lay on my bed and stewed in my despair.

I knew that Gurdjieff's teaching was my salvation, but I just couldn't break the code of his teaching of "work on oneself." What the hell did that mean?

I lay on my bed in silence. Then, at the foot of my bed, just above my eye level, a tiny dot of blue light appeared in midair. I stared incredulously. Then the tiny dot of blue light expanded to form a perfect donut-shaped circle about three feet in diameter with a hole in the center. Too stunned to be startled, I just stared at the blue circle. Then a tiny dot of yellow light appeared inside the ring at the top of the circle, and it then expanded to form a straight line inside the ring, then it stopped, made a right angle and formed another straight line, then another right angle and another straight line, and another right angle and then another straight line and it formed a perfect square of yellow light within the circle of blue light. I couldn't believe my eyes.

There, at the foot of my bed, suspended in midair, was a circle of blue light that had just been miraculously "squared" by a yellow light!

It took years before I learned that this was what Carl Jung would have called my personal mandala which symbolized that one day I would do the impossible and give birth to my spiritual self. In the archetypal manifestation of the "squared circle" I foresaw my own spiritual destiny; but I had no idea what I had just witnessed. *To me it was not a spontaneous symbolic eruption of my creative unconscious, but a paranormal experience that I regarded with the reverence of a divine miracle!*

19. The Family Shadow

"As far as we can discern," wrote C. G. Jung, "the sole purpose of human existence is to kindle a light in the darkness of mere being. It may even be assumed that just as the unconscious affects us, so the increase in our consciousness affects the unconscious" (*Memories, Dreams, Reflections*, p. 326).

It was inevitable that I find Jung in my journey to "wholeness and singleness of self," because he did more than anyone to make conscious the unconscious nature of man. His depth psychology opened the door to the unconscious, and the dark forces of the human personality that Jung called the *archetypal shadow* no longer bewitch the conscious mind.

That's what Gurdjieff's Work did for me. The harder I "worked" on myself with his teaching, the more light I shone in the darkness of my being. In effect, I made conscious my unconscious *shadow self*; that's why I experienced the "snap" that night while waiting on tables at the Nipigon Inn Hotel as the naked strippers danced on stage.

So intensely did I *non-identify* with my summer cold and naked strippers as I waited on my customers that I transformed enough consciousness with all of my conscious efforts to *non-identify* that I reached the breaking point and something had to give.

I've employed the metaphor of a balloon filled with air until it bursts, because this is precisely what I feel happened to me that night: I had poured so much conscious energy into my unconscious self with all of my concerted efforts to *non-identify* with everything that I did ever since I began living Gurdjieff's teaching after I dropped out of university that when I waited on tables that night and made superhuman efforts to *non-identify* with my cold and naked strippers I literally filled my unconscious self with so much conscious awareness that the archetypal matrix of my unconscious *shadow* had to burst and set me free.

DO WE HAVE AN IMMORTAL SOUL?

That's why I literally felt that "snap" inside me that set me free from the hold my *shadow* had upon me; and as difficult as this may be to believe, I *knew* instantly that I had just liberated myself from the prison of my own falseness...

Once I was set free from the grips of my unconscious false self I was ready for C. G. Jung, whose groundbreaking psychology would help me understand what I had done; that's why the merciful divine law of synchronicity arranged for me to find Jung's teaching through his memoir *Memories, Dreams, Reflections* in one of my favorite little book stores called *The Black Unicorn* in the city of Thunder Bay where I went to university.

I loved the picture of the venerable octogenarian Jung on the cover of his memoir, smoking his pipe as he proofed some pages of his writing; and I devoured his book with no less appetite that I did any book that I had been strongly "nudged" to read.

Jung drew me into his life story because he spoke about his interior life, something that I was very familiar with. Jung did not dwell so much on the outer circumstances of his life, only to give his inner life contextual reference; that's why I fell in love with the man—*because he was driven by his own daemon no less than I was driven by mine!*

I understood that. I knew what it meant to be driven by the irrepressible forces of your own *karmic destiny*, despite the fact that I hadn't yet conceptualized the individuation process of our Soul self; but that's what Jung helped me do: he gave me the words, concepts, and psychological wisdom drawn from his own quest for his lost soul to help me understand my own unfathomably unique individuation process.

And when I devoured *Memories, Dreams, Reflections* I purchased *The Portable Jung,* edited by Joseph Campbell, thus beginning my lifelong study of Jung's teaching that never ceased to amaze me—especially *The Red Book* that Penny purchased for me as a Christmas gift last year from Amazon and which was delivered to our front door by Canpar at 11: 50 A. M. Friday, December 28, 2012 and which I completely consumed by 8:35 A. M. New Year's Day, January 1, 2013. That's how I found Jung...

20. My Karmic Baggage

I had a mysterious personality change in high school. I can't be sure, but I believe it happened in grade ten. I didn't know what happened to me; all I knew was that I wasn't the same person after it happened. I was the same but different, and this bedeviled me for years until I liberated myself from myself that night in the Nipigon Inn Hotel.

It didn't happen in one dramatic moment. It happened without noticing that it happened. All I experienced were the mysterious effects of what happened to me, and it took many years before I understood this change in my personality; and I have to thank C. G. Jung for helping me resolve the mystery of my *archetypal shadow self.*

When I heard the voice in my mind ask me *"why do you lie?"* I did not know that this question was my key to personal freedom that I experienced that night waiting on tables when I pushed myself to the point of "snapping" myself free of the unconscious hold that my *archetypal shadow* had upon me; but that's what happened.

I was an unconscious liar because sometime in grade ten my center of gravity shifted from my conscious personality to the unconscious *shadow* side of my personality, and I became a prisoner of the *non-being* aspect of my nature, which was the repressed and unresolved aspect of my personality—i. e., my inauthentic, *shadow self.*

This doesn't mean that I behaved any more unconsciously than the miserable Hollywood director in my dream who was firmly ensconced in his *non-being*; I was just as conscious as before, but now that my center of gravity had shifted to my inauthentic self I was not as conscious of myself and was much more easily influenced by my *shadow*, which is why I began to experience a strange and inexplicable impulse to falseness.

I could not explain it, and every time I gave in to this impulse I suffered enormous guilt and shame. I became a very conflicted young man, and although I got away with it more often than not (which did not mean that people could not see my inauthenticity; many did and called me "phony"), I got caught sometimes; like the time I got caught cheating playing pool with friends after school, which we did often.

The game we played was called "pea pool," formally known as Kelly pool. Fifteen pea-shaped little round black wooden balls with printed numbers are shaken in a leather pouch and each player is given a number which he does not show to anyone. Then someone shoots the cue ball and scatters the racked fifteen numbered billiard balls on the pool table and players take turns shooting the balls into the pockets, starting from number one and on up until they miss and the next player in the given order shoots next; and when the ball that has your number is pocketed, you are out of the game. The person who pockets his ball wins the game and prize money.

Well, I managed to deceive the other players by having the advantage of concealing two or three "peas" in separate pant and/or shirt pockets. For example, I would put number four in the right front pocket of my pants; number seven in the left front pocket; and number nine in one of my back pockets. This gave me much better odds of being the last person standing. I cheated like this for weeks; but I pushed my luck too far and got caught with four "peas" in my pockets when one person suspected something wasn't kosher and he caught me checking my different pockets and I had to suffer my humiliation for years.

One day I may have the courage to write a story on this ignominious experience that went a long way to making my high school life more miserable than it already was, but suffice to say now that that impulse to falseness bedeviled me for years until I finally broke the beast's back that night in the Nipigon Inn Hotel; and I have Carl Jung to thank for my understanding of what today has become identified as *"the shadow effect"*—that devastating experience when one's *shadow* comes out to sabotage one's life. As Debbie Ford said, "Our *shadow* incites us to act out in ways we never imagined we could and to waste our vital energy on bad habits and repetitive behaviors. Our *shadow* keeps us from full self-expression, from speaking our truth, and from living an authentic life," (*The Shadow Effect*, by Debbie Ford, Deepak Chopra, and Marianne Williamson, p. 2).

My unconscious *shadow* began to sabotage my life in high school with my impulse to falseness, which escalated to cheating and deceiving; and it climaxed five or six years later in the overpowering impulse to have a sexual experience one night that so traumatized me that it catapulted me into my quest for my true self, because I knew that the person who did what he did was not the real me; and I vowed to find my true self or die trying.

21. Are We Nothing but Soul Soup?

This question of whether we have an immortal soul or not is directly related to the natural process of individuation. I've come to believe that we, meaning humankind, are no different than any other living organism on earth; we all evolve from seeds.

The acorn seed has to evolve into an oak tree; the tomato seed has to evolve into a tomato plant; and the apple seed has to evolve into an apple tree. All seeds evolve into what they have been genetically programmed by nature to evolve into. As Jung put it during an interview late in his life, with that impish twinkle in his eyes, "The acorn cannot evolve into a monkey. It must evolve into an oak tree."

So the question that I've asked myself is this: what does man evolve into?

We all ask the question, "who am I?" But what do we mean by "who?" Is not this "who" the core of our own identity that we have yet to realize? Is this why we don't know who we are, because we have not yet realized who we are? At what point can the acorn seed say that it is an oak tree? This is our dilemma...

I was listening to a writer on a radio program online the other night talking about her novels on reincarnation. She was asked by the host about her belief in reincarnation. Her belief was essentially Buddhist; meaning, when we die our essence-energy goes into a kind of "soul soup" (she quoted Deepak Chopra), so when we are reborn we are made up of this "soul soup"—which means, according to this perspective, that we are all a blend of everyone's essential nature, and we don't have a *core identity*—an autonomous self.

In so much that we are all an essential part of life, I don't disagree with this Buddhist perspective; because life is energy, and we are all made up of life-energy. But this does not explain the natural impulse that we all have to individuate and realize who we are; otherwise why would we continue to ask the question "who am I?"

OREST STOCCO

It just seems to me that the Buddhist perspective fails to acknowledge our greatest need in life, which is to realize our *core identity* that has taken millions of years of natural evolution to give birth to; otherwise why would the ancient alchemists say that we have to complete what nature has left unfinished?

What has nature left unfinished if not the evolution of our *core identity*? Nature has taken us (our *core identity*) as far as she possible can according to the laws that govern natural evolution, but to complete what nature cannot finish we have to transcend these laws of natural evolution; and this is what the Way according to Gurdjieff was all about, and the Way according to Jesus, and the Way according to Gnosticism, Alchemy, and Taoism—the Way, period; because the Way is the path to "wholeness and singleness of self."

In effect, all paths lead to the Way; this is why Gurdjieff said that there is only self-initiation into the mysteries of life. And since the Way *is* life, then there is only self-initiation into the Way. So whether we know it or not, every path in some measure initiates us into the Way; until one day we wake up to the Way, as I did with Gurdjieff's teaching.

What bothers me about the Buddhist perspective on reincarnation is the denial of the natural impulse to individuate our *core identity* which has taken eons to realize through the natural process of karmic evolution. For the Buddhist, reincarnation is not a question of an autonomous soul being born again, but of the "soul soup" taking on a new life; so when a person is hypnotically regressed to their past lives, for example, it is not their own individuating *core identity* that they recall in their past-life regression, but the identity of an essential someone in the "soul soup" which may or may not be one's former life.

In *The Monk and the Philosopher*, Tibetan monk Matthieu Ricard calls this "soul soup" the "continuum of consciousness." This "continuum of consciousness" is made up of the essential nature of life, which includes humankind; and out of this "continuum of consciousness" we are reborn—but not as an individuating autonomous soul, only as a "separate stream" of this "continuum of consciousness."

Again, I don't disagree with this perspective, and I know it seems like I'm dancing around the mulberry bush; but I want to make

60

it crystal clear that as right as the Buddhist perspective may be, because essentially we are all an aspect of this "continuum of consciousness," we are also an individuating, autonomous Soul self.

This is what I'm trying to illustrate with this essay on how I came to the realization of my *core identity*, by pointing out that we individuate in our *core identity* from one lifetime to the next according to our past-life karmic history.

22. The Genesis of Life on Planet Earth

I had an experience several years after I left university and started my own contract painting business that took me more than thirty years to understand; and only because of what I experienced when I had seven past-life regressions.

As fantastic as it was, I had absolutely no idea how pivotal this experience would be to understanding the meaning and purpose of life; nor did I even begin to imagine how it would help resolve the question of consciousness that preoccupies quantum physics today.

In his book *The Self-Aware Universe, How Consciousness Creates the Material World,* quantum physicist Dr. Amit Goswami asks the question: "Maybe if we find out how the individual "I" arises, we will be able to understand ourselves better?" (p. 162)

After some brilliant reasoning, Dr. Goswami comes to the startling paradigm-shifting conclusion that "the self of self-reference and the consciousness of the original consciousness, together, make what we call self-consciousness ...As the romantic poet John Keats intuited: 'See the world if you please /As a vale for soulmaking.' Without the immanent world of manifestation, there would be no soul, no self that experiences itself as separate from the object it perceives" (Ibid p. 188).

In what is probably his most insightful letter to his brother, John Keats wrote: "There may be intelligences or sparks of divinity in millions, but they are not Souls till they acquire identities, till each one is personally itself. Intelligences are atoms of perception—they know and they see and they are pure; in short, they are God. How then are Souls to be made? How then are these sparks which are God to have identity given them—so as to possess a bliss peculiar to each one by individual existence? How but by the medium of a world like this?" (*Values*, p. 12, edited by J. G. Bennet, a lifelong student of Gurdjieff's teaching). With poetic genius, John Keats caught a glimpse of the Divine Plan of God—the natural process of individuating the consciousness of God, which he called Soul making.

DO WE HAVE AN IMMORTAL SOUL?

I was living Gurdjieff's teaching (as well as my *Royal Dictum*) with passionate intensity when I had the miraculous experience that gave me my first glimpse of the Divine Plan of God, but aside from the mind-blowing effect that it had upon me I had absolutely no idea what this experience meant. I had a lot of conscious individuating ("dying before dying") to do before I initiated myself into the divine mystery of consciousness.

There I was, then; sitting in the back yard of my parents home, nicely protected from the wind, the spring sun warming my face and body. It had been a long winter, as they usually are in Northwestern Ontario, and it felt good to bask in the warm spring sun; so I leaned my chair back and let my head rest upon the stucco wall of the house.

God, it felt good to soak in the warm spring sun; and I basked in the moment's glory without any thought on my mind, just a quiet, comforting feeling of *just being*. I don't know how long I sat like this, but I began to feel myself floating back through time.

I began to go back slowly, gradually, a week, a month, a year, many years, a century, further and further back, thousands of years, faster and faster, all the way back to when there was absolutely no life on the earth at all, which I observed from a vantage point above the earth. Planet Earth was barren. Dull, grey, and completely barren of all life.

And I saw the gases of Planet Earth rise, and as the gases rose they blended with the gases of the sky; and when they blended they formed amino acids, the first building blocks of life—and that's when it happened: *the moment the gasses blended I felt myself enter into the first building blocks of life and I experienced the genesis of life on Planet Earth!*

I *knew* the moment I slipped into the first building blocks of life (I learned many years later from watching a science documentary on TV that the first building blocks of life are made up of amino acids), that I *animated* the life process; but it was so mind-blowing to realize that *I* was responsible for jump-starting the life process that I couldn't bear to think about it, and I simply stored that experience in the back of my mind.

It's hard to describe what it felt like to just slip into the life process at its very inception; but I had an experience once waking up from a dream that comes close to what happened when I slipped into the amino acids to *animate* the life process.

My dream was memorable because it had to do with my karmic destiny. In my dream I'm with four or five older male souls who are counselling me on my decision to change the course of my life. I wanted to get out of the contract painting business and go into another type of business, a drive-in restaurant that I was looking into buying at the time.

My counselors on the other side strongly objected to my decision. They told me that I still had a lot to learn from my contract painting business, and they insisted that I not change the course of my karmic destiny; and I woke up from my dream.

But it was the way that I woke up that made my dream so memorable: I felt myself slip back into my physical body, just as I had slipped into the first building blocks of life; but in this case it was like slipping into a suit of clothing. In one quick liquid motion I slipped back in my body, which was sound asleep, and I woke up fully aware of slipping back into my body with the memory of my experience on the other side completely intact.

I was not happy with the counsel I had just received on the other side, and I went ahead with my plan to buy the drive-in restaurant anyway; but by some bizarre twist of fate I lost the deal to my flaky cousin who a few years earlier had introduced me to my new spiritual path, and it took years before I could bring myself to forgive her betrayal.

The owner of the drive-in and I had shaken hands on the deal, but by some strange quirk of fate, which I now attribute to mischievous intervention, I just happened to be in the wrong place at the wrong time when my flaky cousin snatched the deal away from me; and the only way to do the weird synchronicity responsible for losing the deal would be to work out the full context in a short story. The theme of my story would be the *Trickster effect*—a mysterious archetypal manifestation not unlike the *shadow effect.*

The *Archetypal Trickster* is the unpredictable, playful, and sometimes quite mischievous side of the synchronicity principle that comes into play in our life when we refuse to do what we're supposed to do to stay on our destined course; and because of the *Trickster effect,* I was forced to stay on course to learn the lessons that I needed to learn in my contract painting and drywall taping business, which I continued to do until I had bypass surgery some fifteen years later when Penny and I relocated to Georgian Bay.

And the reason I had to stay on my destined course was because this course would lead to my seven past-life regressions that I had in Georgian Bay, which led me to meet the medium who channeled St. Padre Pio who helped resolve my deep-seated karmic issues with my Roman Catholic faith; so as much as I believe that we have the freedom to choose our own path in life, sometimes our path is forced upon us.

23. Consciousness Is Sui Generis

As Dr. Amit Goswami makes clear in *The Self-Aware Universe*, "the self of self-reference and the consciousness of the original consciousness, together, make what we call self-consciousness." This was my experience of slipping into the amino acids and jump-starting the life process on Planet Earth, but it would take many years before I made sense of this miraculous event; and as much as I would love to explain how I came to my realization of the Divine Plan of God after I had my seven past-life regressions, I'm not at liberty to show my cards just yet because the creative dialectic is still in play...

Consciousness is not an epiphenomenon; it is *sui generis*. This is what Dr. Amit Goswami, professor of physics at the University of Oregon for over thirty years, proves with his book *The Self-Aware Universe;* but his proof is theoretical.

Dr. Eben Alexander, a skeptical neurosurgeon firmly entrenched in the materialist philosophy of life, had a harrowing experience that proved that consciousness is not an epiphenomenon of the brain, which he shared with the world in his remarkable book *Proof of Heaven. A Neurosurgeon's Journey into the Afterlife;* but I didn't need any more anecdotal evidence that we are all sparks of divine consciousness. I read *Proof of Heaven* because I love conversion experience stories, my favorite being Dr. Brian L. Weiss's story which he shared in his ground-breaking memoir *Many Lives, Many Masters.*

A conversion experience story is a story of one's conversion from belief to non-belief, or from non-belief to belief. One of the most dramatic conversion stories of belief to non-belief that I came across was the groundbreaking Christian evangelist Charles Templeton's story of his belief in God to non-belief in God that he shared with the world in his memoir *Farewell to God.* Charles Templeton was a contemporary of Billy Graham, and together they helped launch the fundamentalist Christian movement in North

America; but Templeton suffered a crisis in faith and went from one extreme to the other.

And social activist/author June Callwood, a founding member of Casey House in Toronto (named after her son), also had a dramatic albeit private conversion from belief in God to non-belief in God. When her son was killed by a drunk driver, she went to church and knelt for six hours asking God why her son had been taken away from her so young and so tragically; but she heard nothing. "There was nothing there," she said, and she got up and left the Church and God and never looked back.

Many years later, just before her death of cancer at the age of 82, "St. June," as she was called (because she had been dubbed "the conscience of Toronto" for her good works) was asked if she believed in God and an afterlife. She did not. "I believe in kindness," she said. "That's what will save the world." But her conversion story, as moving as it was, brought tears to my eyes; not for her relentless good works, but for her tortured unbelief.

And then there's Doctor Eben Alexander's conversion story which brought me to tears of joy. He believed that the brain created consciousness, and when the body dies so does our personal identity; but "on November 10, 2008, however, at age fifty-four, my luck seemed to run out. I was struck by a rare illness and thrown into a coma for seven days. During that time, my entire neocortex—the outer surface of the brain, the part that makes us human—was shut down. Inoperative. In essence, absent," he writes in *Proof of Heaven*; and then he puts on record what he believed about consciousness and personal identity before he contracted a rare illness and had his remarkable near-death conversion experience:

"When your brain is absent, you are absent, too. As a neurosurgeon, I'd heard many stories over the years of people who had strange experiences, usually after suffering cardiac arrest: stories of travelling to mysterious, wonderful landscapes; of talking to dead relatives—even of meeting God Himself.

"Wonderful stuff, no question. But all of it, in my opinion, was pure fantasy. What caused the otherworldly types of experiences that such people so often report? I didn't claim to know, but I did know that they were brain-based. All of consciousness is. If you don't have a working brain, you can't be conscious.

"This is because the brain is the machine that produces consciousness in the first place. When the machine breaks down, consciousness stops...or so I would have told you before my own brain crashed.

"During my coma my brain was working improperly—it wasn't working *at all*. I now believe that this might have been what was responsible for the depth and intensity of the near-death experience (NDE) that I myself underwent during it...I was encountering the reality of a world of consciousness that existed completely free of the limitations of my physical brain. Mine was in some ways a perfect storm of near-death-experiences. (*Proof of Heaven*, pp. 8-9)

From a non-believer to a believer, Dr. Alexander is now on a mission to prove to the world that consciousness is not an epiphenomenon of the brain, and that our personal identity exists independent of our brain; but of all the conversion stories that I have come across, the one I love most is Dr. Brian L. Weiss's conversion from non-belief in reincarnation to belief in reincarnation, and I love it most because I just know that it was initiated with delicious mischievousness by the *Archetypal Trickster.*

In *Many Lives, Many Masters* Dr. Weiss tells of the strange serendipitous events that brought his patient Catherine to him for her anxiety and panic attacks, and the serendipitous way that he learned about reincarnation when under hypnosis he inadvertently gave her an open-ended command to "go back to the time from when your symptoms arise," fully expecting her to go back to her early childhood but instead goes back to a past lifetime.

"I was stunned," he writes. "Previous lifetimes? Reincarnation? My clinical mind told me that she was not fantasizing this material, that she was not making this up...My gut reaction was that I had stumbled upon something I knew very little about— reincarnation and past-life memories. It couldn't be, I told myself; my scientifically trained mind resisted it. Yet here it was, happening before my eyes. I couldn't explain it, but I couldn't deny the reality of it either." (*Many Lives, Many Masters*, pp. 27, 29)

DO WE HAVE AN IMMORTAL SOUL?

Today Dr. Weiss is one of the world's most successful past-life regression therapists, conducting workshops all over the world!

24. The Three Circles of Life

If we do not have an autonomous soul, why do people remember their past lives? But before I address this question, I'd like to address a more fundamental question that has taken me the better part of my life to answer: *why do some people believe in God and an afterlife and others don't?*

Many brilliant people don't believe in God and an afterlife. The exceptionally brilliant mathematician/philosopher Bertrand Russell did not; and neither did Sartre, Camus, and Schopenhauer. Whether Nietzsche did nor not is open to question, but either way; why do some of the world's best minds not believe in God and an afterlife?

As I said earlier when I addressed my interest in Sartre and Camus, they got trapped by the dynamic consciousness of their *being* and *non-being* and could not transcend the existential dimension of their ego self; so they could not fathom existence beyond what they experienced with their senses. For them, consciousness was an epiphenomenon of the brain, and when the body died so did their personal identity. But Dr. Eben Alexander's remarkable NDE has proven that this is not the case; so why do skeptics continue to disbelieve?

The answer is very simple, but it is also so philosophically abstract that it would be easy to dismiss. Nonetheless, it satisfied my curiosity when I finally worked it out; and it has to do with the mystical nature of consciousness and the self.

Without going into how I came to this realization (which I will do when I'm called upon to show my cards), during my long and anguishing self-initiation into the mysteries of life I came to see that the self is a unit of self-aware consciousness that has taken nature millions of years to give birth to; and this unit of self-consciousness goes through three stages to complete its divinely encoded purpose— the *exoteric*, *mesoteric*, and *esoteric* stages of evolution; or, the outer, middle, and inner stages of self-realization consciousness.

DO WE HAVE AN IMMORTAL SOUL?

In the Divine Plan of God, life evolves through the process of natural selection until one species constellates enough consciousness of life to become aware of itself as a separate unit of consciousness from the rest of life; and this new-born "I" continues to evolve from one lifetime to the next through the *exoteric first stage*, which is governed by the laws of karma and reincarnation, until it is evolved enough in self-awareness to enter the *mesoteric second stage* of evolution where it will take evolution into its own hands to complete what nature cannot finish; meaning, the "I" has to take responsibility for its own karma to complete nature's obligation, which is to realize "singleness and wholeness of self."

In short, the reflective self evolves through the *exoteric first stage* of evolution unaware of the law of karma that governs its growth in life; but when the reflective self has evolved enough to become aware that karma governs its life, one begins to look for the Way which will liberate them from the eternal cycle of *being* and *becoming*.

This brings them to the *mesoteric second stage* of evolution, where they are introduced to the Way by the natural process of life (*when the student is ready, the teacher appears*); which simply means that they will be introduced to the path best suited to their state of consciousness (as I was at various times in my life), and one then lives the Way consciously by taking responsibility for their personal karma.

And as one lives the Way consciously one transforms their consciousness and transcend their *exoteric* ego-self, as I did with my personal path that I forged out of Gurdjieff's teaching, my *Royal Dictum,* the sayings of Jesus, and other gems of golden wisdom; and after considerable effort, which may take many more lifetimes, one will transcend their ego-self and give birth to their spiritual self and they will be ready for the third and final stage of evolution in their "wholeness and singleness of self."

What determines whether one believes in God and an afterlife then is determined by the three stages of evolution; the *exoteric*, *mesoteric*, and *esoteric* stage. The *exoteric* stage is characterized by the dynamic process of *being* and *becoming*; which is the existential consciousness of life and death, and as long as one is going through the *exoteric first stage* of evolution one will always have doubts about

God and the afterlife; and not until one transcends the *exoteric* consciousness of life and death will they begin to see the spiritual reality of eternal life beyond the endless cycle of *being* and *becoming—because as long as we are still becoming we will never know for certain that we are eternal Soul.*

That's what brought me to Pythagoras in my Greek lifetime. I heard whispers and rumors in Athens that he possessed a secret knowledge of life, and I wanted to know why a flower could die at the end of summer and come back to life in the spring. What was this impenetrable mystery of the permanence of life within the impermanence of life?

This was the divine mystery of Soul; and Pythagoras initiated me into the secret doctrine of reincarnation and teachings of the Way that would help me break the recurring cycle of *being* and *becoming*. But it would take many more lifetimes before I would bring my karmic destiny into agreement with my spiritual destiny and finally break the cycle.

25. The Two Paths of Life

To be clear, then; as long as one's "I" is centered in the existential dynamic of the *exoteric* circle of life, the *being* and *becoming* stage of the natural process of self-realization consciousness, one can never be certain of his essential nature, or Soul self if you will—because the consciousness of *being* and *becoming* is an existential consciousness of life and death, not a spiritual consciousness of "life everlasting," to use Christ's phrase.

I don't want to get caught up in the dialectic of the *being* and *becoming* aspect of the individuation process of our essential nature, but because I was fortunate enough to awaken to how the Way works in life I began to "see" the *shadow* side of our ego-personality, and as difficult as it may be to comprehend (because it defies natural logic), the *shadow* side of our personality is made up of the consciousness of *non-being*, which is the existential consciousness of *becoming* and essentially non-real.

In effect, our unconscious *shadow self* is not real until it *becomes* real in our conscious personality; and it *becomes* real through the natural process of life by the creation and resolution of karma. Karma is the energy of life that we individuate through our life experiences; and depending upon the nature of our karma we are more centered in the *being* aspect or *non-being* aspect of our nature.

In other words, the nature of our experiences determines the ontology of our karma—or the *being* and *non-being* aspect of our nature. Good, positive karma equals *being*, and bad, negative karma equals *non-being*. Positive karma equals *essence*, and negative karma equals *personality*. This is the natural process of individation in the *exoteric* circle of life. We grow in *essence* or *personality* according to the karma that we create; so the more karmically resolved we are, the more we are centered in the *being* aspect of our nature and the more authentic we are, and the less karmically resolved we are, the more we are centered in the *non-being* aspect of our nature and the less authentic we are.

Like the two Hollywood directors of my dream, for example; one was centered in the *being* aspect of his nature and was more genuine and authentic than the other who was centered in the *non-being* aspect of his nature. One director was working his way into the *mesoteric* circle of life, and the other was firmly ensconced in the *exoteric* circle of life; which made one more of a believer in eternal life than the other. In Christ's terms, one heard the call and was on his way to being chosen; and the other was deaf to the call.

Having said this, we can see what it means to take evolution into our own hands to complete what nature cannot finish. In the *exoteric* circle of life we are not conscious of the law of karma that determines our destiny (*"we are condemned to be free,"* as Sartre concluded); and not until we have evolved enough to see that we are responsible for the karma that writes the script of our life will we be ready to enter the *mesoteric* second stage and take evolution into our own hands (*we are free to be condemned,* as I came to realize). And we will know when we are ready for the *mesoteric* circle of life when we can no longer suffer the *unbearable longing* of our Soul self; like Jung, for example.

John Freeman, who interviewed Carl Jung on October 22, 1959 for the BBC Face to Face documentary, asked Jung a question that reveals where Jung was centered at that time of his young life, which was the *being* aspect of his nature.

"Now, can you take me back to your childhood?" asks Freeman. "Do you remember the occasion when you first felt conscious of your own individual self?"

And Jung replies: "This was in my eleventh year. There I suddenly was on my way to school I stepped out of a mist. It was just as if I had been in a mist, walking in a mist, and I stepped out of it and I knew, 'I am what I am.' And then I thought, 'But what have I been before?' And then I found that I had been in a mist not knowing how to differentiate myself from things. I was just one thing among other things."

At the age of eleven Carl Jung experienced the *being* aspect of his nature which he conceptualized when he said "I am what I am." But then he got caught up in the *becoming* aspect of his nature and began to individuate his identity by devoting himself to his medical studies and graduating and obtaining a position as assistant physician at the Bergholzli psychiatric hospital in Zurich where under the directorship of Dr. Eugen Bleuler he was initiated into the dark and impenetrable mysteries of the human psyche.

He then became a disciple of Dr. Sigmund Freud and psychoanalysis, but because he could not agree with some of Freud's fundamental premises he was forced by the integrity of his own *daemonically*-driven desire to understand the human psyche to break away from Freud and initiate his own branch of psychoanalysis, which he called analytical psychology; and he poured his heart and soul into his work. And then came what he called his "confrontation with the unconscious," which changed the course of his life.

Jung recorded his dramatic "confrontation with the unconscious" in a series of black notebooks, which he later transcribed into what he came to call *Liber Novus*, now famously known as *The Red Book*; and he begins his hero's journey into the unconscious by confessing the loss of his own soul:

"When I had the vision of the flood in October of the year 1913, it happened at a time that was significant for me as a man. At that time, in the fortieth year of my life, I had achieved honor, power, wealth, knowledge, and every human happiness. Then my desire for the increase of these trappings ceased, and the desire ebbed from me and horror came upon me. The vision of the flood seized me and I felt the spirit of the depths, but I did not understand him. Yet he drove me on with *unbearable inner longing* and I said: 'My soul, where are you? Do you hear me? I speak. I call you—are you there? I have returned. I am here again. I have shaken the dust of all the lands from my feet, and I have come to you. I am with you. After long years of long wandering, I have come to you again. Should I tell you everything I have seen, experienced, and drunk in? Or do you want to hear about all the noise of life and the world? But one thing you must know: the one thing I have learned is that one must live this life. *This life is the way, the long sought-after way to the unfathomable, which we call divine. There is no other way, all other ways are false paths.*" (*The Red Book, Liber Novus*, A Reader's Edition, pp. 127-8, italics mine)

C. G. Jung, like many highly accomplished people in the world, was so driven to realize success in his field that he disconnected with his inner, Soul self; and when he could no longer satisfy his longing to *become* ("my desire for the increase of these trappings ceased, and the desire ebbed from me and horror came upon me"), he knew it was time to reconnect with his Soul self; or, to express this *unbearable longing* in the more dramatic language of the hero's journey found in literature (Dante's *Divine Comedy*, Goethe's *Faust*, and Robert Pirsig's *Zen and the Art of Motorcycle Maintenance*), Jung heard the call and went on a quest for his own lost soul. And where did he go to look for his lost soul?

In the depths of his own unconscious…

26. Meeting Carl Gustav Jung

The *exoteric* egoic outer life of the Soul no longer satisfied Jung's longing to become what he longed to be, and he became possessed by an *"unbearable inner longing"* to reconnect with his Soul self; which meant that he was ready to be initiated into the mysteries of the Way in the *mesoteric* circle of life. This is why Jung became so absorbed by the Gnostic teachings first and then the cryptic writings of the Alchemists; both secret teachings of the Way that he desperately needed to reconnect with his Soul self.

I met Carl Jung in a dream. He read my book *The Way of Soul* and wanted to talk to me about what he called "the alpha and omega of the self" that was the essential theme of my book. The curious thing was however, my book *The Way of Soul* was not yet published out here. In fact, it wasn't even transcribed from my tapes. But over there, on the other side, Jung held a copy in his hand and wanted to discuss it with me.

I had enormous love and respect for Carl Jung, and I could not get over how privileged I felt to meet him in my dream. He looked as he did when he was interviewed by John Freeman two years before he died—wise, venerable, and endearingly humble; but so animated was he by my book *The Way of Soul* that his piercing small eyes, which reflected a mischievous hint of deviltry, still shone with the fire of his unrequited desire to solve the central mystery of his life—the mystery of "the alpha and omega of the self."

And I just loved listening to him. Jung was the only person I had ever meaningfully conversed with who had *become* the consciousness of his knowledge; and by this I mean that Jung *was* what he knew (and he knew so much he could be intimidating), which differentiated him from most people who only have an intellectual understanding of what they know. There was a chasm of difference, of which he was completely conscious.

Because I had crossed this mysterious chasm (from *personality* to *essence*), we had a meeting of minds; but I intrigued

Jung. He could not fathom how I had managed to "pull it off," as he put it. Jung loved to use American slang, and by "pulling it off" he meant that he couldn't quite fathom how I had managed to do the impossible and realize my Soul self, as I had been foretold by my own unconscious with the symbolic "squaring of the circle" mandala that manifested before my eyes in my second year at university.

It actually bothered him; but in a good way. "You can see my quandary?" he said to me, wrinkling his octogenarian brow. After all, it took Jung his whole life before he learned from his dream just a few days before he died that he had realized "wholeness and singleness of self," so he knew the price that he had to pay to reclaim his lost soul. That's why shortly before his death he said to Miguel Serrano (*C. G. Jung and Herman Hesse, A Record of Two Friendships*), "The path is very difficult."

We both knew what "the path" was, but he couldn't figure out how I had managed to break the code of the Way which took him years of studious ferreting through ancient Gnostic and Alchemical texts to capture (not to mention decoding his own historic "confrontation with the unconscious"), and I both excited and bedeviled him.

That's why he came to me in my dream; he had to meet me in person. And we talked for what seemed as long if not longer than his famous talk with Freud when they met for the first time—thirteen hours. But I need not go into our talk here, which I've done in my novel *The Waking Dream;* suffice to say that Jung and I had a meeting of minds, which hopefully I'll get to expound upon one day when I write my book *The Beauty of Suffering* that came to me in a synoptic vision when Jesus said to Philemon at the end of *The Red Book, 'I bring to you the beauty of suffering. That is what is needed by whoever hosts the worm."*

The stage of my novel *The Way of Soul* was set into motion by my synchronized relationship with a water color artist whom I call Kevin Archer in *The Waking Dream*. I met Kevin in Creemore, Ontario on a job that I was doing. Kevin was in a spiritual quandary: his art had brought him to a dead end, and he fell into a state of post-creative despair.

DO WE HAVE AN IMMORTAL SOUL?

I gave him my novel memoir to read, *What Would I Say Today If I Were to Die Tomorrow?* My novel spoke to him, and we connected on a Soul to Soul level; that's what initiated my bold experiment in what Carl Jung called "active imagination."

This is a mystifying and dangerous exercise; but all creative writers practice it when they engage in the process of writing a novel, and all artists when they get caught up in their own creative process. They can't explain it, but they connect with the creative unconscious and their work becomes ensouled with what Jung called "the spirit of the depths."

Kevin had been called, but he didn't know where to turn to reconnect with his Soul self; and that's when the merciful law of divine synchronicity introduced me into his life—*once again proving that when the student is ready, the teacher appears.* And every time we met in Creemore, Kevin drew the Way out of me with such fluidity that it inspired me to initiate my "Soul talk books," beginning with *The Way of Soul.*

It's difficult to explain the *special connection* that Kevin and I had. I knew that he had been called to the Way so he could reconnect with his Soul self and continue painting, which up to that point had satisfied his inner longing to be an artist; and because I was *conscious* of how the Way worked in life, I was compelled by the Divine Law of the Way to pass on my *gnosis of the Way* to help him reconnect with his "inner artist."

This is all in *The Waking Dream*, so I need not expound upon it here; suffice to say that I did not want to stem the flow of *virtue* that Kevin drew out of me after he reconnected with his "inner artist" and moved on with his life (I haven't seen him since, but I'm sure that when he comes to another spiritual impasse a new teacher will appear to assist him on his journey to "singleness and wholeness of self"), so I decided to try something very bold, very adventurous —*to let go and let Soul speak into my recorder!*

If I may. Whenever Kevin and I met he always had a pressing *need to know.* He could not define what he hungered to *know*, just that there was *something* that he just had to *know*; and invariably at some point in our conversation we connected in that *special way* and my *gnosis of the Way* poured out of me in a stream of such poignantly relevant information that it always satisfied Kevin's *need to know.*

And the next time we met the same thing happened again; and his inner, compulsive *need to know* was satisfied once more by the *virtue* that he drew out of me. Finally his *need to know* was satisfied enough to reconnect him with his "inner artist" and he was back on his karmically destined path of his heart's desire, and we parted company; but I loved so much how the Way poured out of me whenever we connected in that *special way* that I had to continue the creative connection with my Higher Self. That's what initiated my three "Soul talk" books, starting with *The Way of Soul.*

Every morning on my hour-long commute to my work in Creemore, I let go and "let Soul talk" into my mini recorder that I had hanging off my rearview mirror; and on my way back home I did the same, and after my job was finished I continued my exercise in "active imagination" until I "Soul talked" three books into my recorder; but I never got around to transcribing my tapes. That's why I was so astonished to learn that *The Way of Soul* was published on the other side and that it excited Carl Jung's interest enough to want to talk with me. *And we met in my dream…*

27. Shattering the Glass Darkly

Although *The Waking Dream* was set into motion with my *special relationship* with Kevin Archer, it was literally inspired by an incredible experience I had one day when I came home from my call to Midhurst just north of Barrie, Ontario one Sunday morning where I had gone to give an estimate for a painting job. I brought my recorder with me, and on en route I "Soul talked" the last chapter of my book *The Soul of Happiness.*

I was so charged with creative energy from "Soul talking" my last chapter that Penny felt my energy the moment I walked into the house. She said it hit her like a powerful wave and nearly knocked her over. She made us a late breakfast, and then I went into the living room to read my Sunday paper; and that's when it happened.

I rested my stocking feet on the brass rim of our round smoked glass coffee table and read the paper in relaxed comfort. After Penny did the dishes she came over and joined me with her cup of coffee. She wasn't there more than a few minutes when the glass of our coffee table imploded and shattered into half a dozen pieces, and we were awestruck.

The brass eagle that Penny had given me for a birthday present years before sank to the floor when the thick smoked glass plate spontaneously imploded and shattered before our eyes, and Penny said to me: *"Oh Orest, what have you done now?"*

Nonplussed, I pleaded my innocence. "I didn't do anything." A moment or so of baffled silence later, I exclaimed: "THAT'S A WAKING DREAM!"

A waking dream is an anomalous experience that happens for a special reason. Edgar Cayce said that dreams "work to accomplish two things. They work to solve the problems of the dreamer's conscious, waking life. And they work to quicken in the dreamer new potentials which are his to claim." Waking dreams do the same thing, only a waking dream does not happen when we are asleep; it happens when we are awake.

So, what "problem" was my waking dream helping me solve? And, much more important, just what caused the thick smoked glass to shatter like that?

I go into detail in my novel, but essentially it was because my energy field was so charged with the creative energy from "Soul talking" the last chapter of my book *The Soul of Happiness* that it poured out of my body through my feet into the brass rim of the coffee table until it was charged enough to skip and charge the brass eagle in the center of the coffee table until both the brass rim and eagle were so charged that they vibrated at such a high frequency that they shattered the thick smoked glass plate—just as an opera singer's voice can reach such a high pitch that it will shatter a champagne glass.

It took a few minutes to unpack my explosive epiphany, but I connected the dots and realized that my waking dream was a spontaneous eruption of my creative unconscious—a material manifestation not unlike the miraculous "squaring of the circle" that I experienced in my second year of university—that symbolically resolved the problem I had posed with the final chapter of my book *The Soul of Happiness.*

The theme of my closing chapter had to do with transforming the consciousness of our ego in order to realize our Soul self. Ego is our mental self, and it is not pure enough in consciousness to transcend the mind (the Mental Plane of Consciousness) and realize our essential nature on the Soul Plane of Consciousness. In effect, ***ego is the mental aspect of our Soul self,*** and it evolves through the *exoteric* circle of the Lower Planes of Consciousness (Physical, Astral, Causal, and Mental Planes) to individuate our Soul self; but because it is not pure enough to realize its Soul nature, it has to be transformed so it can transcend to the Soul Plane where we will realize "wholeness and singleness of self."

Our mind (which is a function of the Mental Plane of Consciousness) is like a "glass darkly" that will not let us see through into the Soul Plane of Consciousness; and to realize our Soul self on the Soul Plane we have to break through the "glass darkly" of our own mind. This was the theme of my closing chapter "The Ontology of Ego." And my waking dream was a symbolic manifestation of the central problem that we all have in life—which is the problem that our ego (mental self) comes to on our journey to "wholeness and singleness of self" and which I resolved by explaining how to transform the impure consciousness of our ego self and break out of the Mental Plane of Consciousness—ergo, my waking dream of shattering the smoked glass of our coffee table which symbolically spoke to shattering the "glass darkly" of the Mental Plane that brought closure to *The Soul of Happiness*; and the following morning I began writing my novel *The Waking Dream.*

28. The Creative Unconscious

To stay connected with my creative unconscious, I continued to practice this amazing exercise of "active imagination," but in a much more contained literary form; I started   writing spiritual musings, beginning with Volume 1: *Just Going with the Flow*; and the following year with Volume 2: *Old Whore Life, Exploring the Shadow Side of Karma*; and the third year with Volume 3: *Stupidity Is Not a Gift of God*.

I've always enjoyed journaling, letter writing, and composing discursive personal essays; and all three genres came together in my spiritual musings, which became my creative way of reflecting upon life from a total personal perspective.

Writing a spiritual musing requires enormous creative discipline, because it's very easy to abandon completely to the creative unconscious; and I have to walk a very fine line between directing the creative process and abandoning to the creative process.

This is difficult to explain; so, if I may, I'd like to illustrate what I mean with an example from my third volume of spiritual musings, *Stupidity Is Not a Gift of God*:

An Exercise in Active Imagination

Today's spiritual musing was born of an exercise in "active imagination," a creative technique that I engage in every so often to play out an idea that craves to be expressed, very much like writing a scene in a novel and giving my characters all the freedom they need to be who they are; and the idea that I wanted to play out was the claim made by a New Age spiritual teaching (the Way of the Eternal) that it is "the most direct path to God."

"That's one perspective," I said, to the short Bette Midler look-alike who made this claim in my imaginary scenario. "It's valid for you, because that's what you choose to believe; but as Neale Donald Walsh said in *Home with God*, his last public conversation with God, 'No path back Home is better than any other.' I know you don't claim this path to be better, only the most direct; but all souls exist in the eternal NOW and are thereby equidistant from God. Given this perspective, no path to God is more direct than any other path; they are all the same distance, if you follow the logic. As God tells Neale, 'Your perspective is your perception.' And by this he meant that what you believe creates your reality. So in the end it all boils down to this: which path is best for me?"

"How would one know that?" a serious-looking lady in her mid-fifties asked. She had come to our monthly spiritual function at the public library of my mind to find out what this "most direct path to God" was all about. A seeker for the last ten years of her life (which began with the accidental drowning of her daughter in the family swimming pool), she never found a path that "spoke" to her, and she was testing the waters one more time. I saw the longing in her eyes, and I felt the anguish of her soul.

"That all depends," I said, and no sooner did I say this and I felt the strongest urge to let Soul speak—which was the whole purpose of my active imagination exercise, to connect with my Higher Self; so I abandoned to my creative unconscious and let Soul say what it had to say to resolve the perplexing issue of finding one's right spiritual path.

"Depends on what?" she asked.

"On how honest you are with yourself," I replied.

"What does that mean?" she asked, with a puzzled look.

"How much do you trust your own intuition?" I answered, and instantly I felt grabbed by the creative impulse of my imagination and I knew that I was in for an exciting new spiritual insight—which was the whole point of my exercise, and the reason why I've come to believe that the creative act of the imagination is the most natural and satisfying path to what Carl Jung called "wholeness and singleness of self."

The lady stared at me, too puzzled to be offended by the implication of my comment that she was not honest enough with herself to find the right path. "I don't see the connection," she said. "Are you saying—*what are you saying, exactly?*"

I smiled at her confusion. "In my book *What Would I Say Today If I Were to Die Tomorrow?* I wrote, **'Self-deception is our**

greatest threat to personal growth, happiness, and wholeness.'
Please don't take this personally, but our capacity for intuitive insight
is directly related to how much we trust ourselves. The less we trust
ourselves, the more confused we're going to be. You asked me how
one would know if a spiritual path is right for them, like this spiritual
path that you came here today to explore; is the Way of the Eternal
right for you or not? Can you tell?"

"Are you asking me?"

"Yes."

"I'm not sure. I haven't made up my mind yet."

"And how would you make up your mind? I presume this isn't
the first spiritual teaching that you've looked into?"

"No. I've looked into many teachings."

"And you haven't found a path you like yet?"

"Not yet."

"So you're still looking; why?"

"None of the paths that I looked into spoke to me."

"And by that I take it to mean that you didn't hear what you
needed to hear to satisfy the longing you have in your soul?"

"That's a good way of putting it. No, I didn't hear what I
needed to hear."

"Obviously, it's a question of resonance. Does a path resonate
with you or not? This speaks to the Sufi saying that there are as many
paths to God as there are souls of man. This means that every soul is
its own path home to God, but a person has to connect with their inner
self to find their path; and that's what the quest for spiritual paths is
all about—finding out which path will help you connect with your
inner self."

"That's what I'd like to know," said the lady, with a glimmer
of hope in her eyes.

"Have you checked out Carolyn Myss's work?" I asked.

"I've come across her books, but I haven't read her yet.
Why?"

"I'd suggest you start with her book *Sacred Contracts*. It
spells out how you can become conscious of your individual purpose
in life—or sacred contract, as she calls it; because that's what you're
looking for. You want to know what your purpose is; right?"

"Yes, I think so. That's why I'm here. If I may ask you, what path are you on?"

"I embrace all teachings, but this path is my anchor teaching."

"Can you explain that for me, please?" the lady asked, her eyes imploring me.

I smiled at her need to know, and being true to my calling I decided to bare myself to her. "To use your metaphor, this path speaks to me the loudest," I replied; "but that doesn't mean that other paths don't speak to me. Every path speaks the Way; but as Jesus would say, do you have eyes to see? Most people don't, because they're not ready for the Way. That's why Jesus also said, *'Many are called but few are chosen.'* Gurdjieff said that nature will only evolve us so far, and then we have to take evolution into our own hands; which implies that if we're not evolved enough to take evolution into our own hands we will not hear the Way when it speaks to us, regardless which path we look into. And as silly as this may sound, we only hear the Way when we hear it; which is why some people will tell you that they just happened to come upon their path by pure chance. They didn't know it, but they were ready for the Way; and the divine law of synchronicity arranged for them to find their path. That's what happened to me. Not once, but several times."

"I don't understand," said the lady, now more confused than ever.

I tried to explain the mystery of the natural process of individuation: "It all depends upon the individual, but a person can outgrow their path. I found Gurdjieff's teaching while studying philosophy at university; but after living his teaching for a number of years I outgrew it, so the divine law of synchronicity once again arranged for me to find the path best suited to my new state of consciousness. And thirty years later, here I am. That's how life works; when the student is ready, the teacher appears…"

I ended my active imagination exercise and went out to get my weekend papers—the *National Post* and *Globe and Mail*; but on my drive into Midland I reflected on my imaginary scenario, and it all seemed to boil down to a question of self-honesty.

"If we're not honest with ourselves, how can we connect with our inner self?" I reflected; and no sooner did I ask the question and

the archetypal lady seeker popped back into the public library of my mind where we were having our imaginary talk—

"What does that have to do with finding a spiritual path that speaks to me?" she asked, responding to my spontaneous reflection. "I don't see the connection."

I paused to let my mind go blank, and then I let Soul speak: "It has everything to do with it, because if we're not honest with ourselves we can't hear the little voice within. How many times have we been nudged to do something only to regret that we didn't pay attention to our silent little voice? And when we did pay attention, weren't we thankful for paying attention because it proved to be the right thing to do? That little voice within is our higher Self speaking to us, but we can't hear it if we aren't honest with ourselves."

I could feel the lady's unease. "I'm honest with myself," she responded, rather nervously. "If I wasn't, I probably would have fallen for any number of teachings."

"Perhaps," I replied, now in full command of my scenario. "Skepticism can work against you as much as it can work for you. Self-honesty demands a certain responsibility that we may not want to assume, and rather than take on the responsibility demanded of us when we listen to our little voice we may justify ourselves to avoid the responsibility. For example, I was introduced to a spiritual path that proved to be the right path for me, but the only reason I looked into this path was because I had the wisdom to override my ego and listen to my inner voice. Let me explain. I thought that the woman who introduced me to the Way of the Eternal was a genuine flake, so how could I take what she had to say seriously? But I put my ego aside and looked into this path because I was nudged to do so, and wouldn't you know it—*it was exactly the right path for me!* In a word, my little voice insisted that I look into this path, but my ego didn't want me to because it judged this lady to be too idiosyncratic to be taken seriously; and thankfully I listened to my little voice."

This gave my imaginary lady seeker something to think about; but that was only my scenario, conjured up in the womb of my active imagination—*and how real could that be?* That's when synchronicity kicked in to validate my new creative insight...

DO WE HAVE AN IMMORTAL SOUL?

I picked up my papers at the Super Store in Midland, plus a few groceries, and came home. Penny and I had lunch, and then she continued with her housework and I sat on the front deck to "work" my papers, as Penny likes to say because I spend hours reading my weekend papers to stay abreast of the unfolding consciousness of our times—true to the imperative that I got from Jesus in Glenda Green's book *Love without End, Jesus Speaks*: ***"Simply follow life and the living. Do not follow the dead and dying. By this I mean do not adapt to ways of life, structures, ideas, concepts, or businesses which are becoming ineffective and obsolete. Look for new alignments, opportunities, and understandings which refresh your life. The whole universe is built around a priority for life and the living,"*** and I always got fresh ideas and new insights from my weekend papers.

After I finished reading Conrad Black's column in the *National Post* (Saturday, July 20, 2013), which I always go to first because I love to see how he is transforming his life and reclaiming his good name, I perused the paper and came upon an article by Guest Columnist Susan Schwartz titled "Stop Pretending to like asparagus," and there it was—*synchronistic confirmation for my creative insight!*

Susan Schwartz used her dislike of asparagus as her entry point into the cognitive dissonance brought about by lack of self-honesty. "So what else have I lied to myself about?" she asks herself, when she finally owns up to disliking asparagus. "I wonder whether my feelings about asparagus are not emblematic of the way in which I have lived much of my life; not acknowledging my preferences or standing up for what I wanted, for instance. Pretending. Acting as if I found people's behavior acceptable when I did not: People said or did things I found hurtful and I would rarely speak up. ***I was deaf to the voice inside trying to guide me. Or if I heard it, I ignored it"*** (bold italics mine).

And to press the point, the divine law of synchronicity gave me all the information I needed to validate my new creative insight about self-honesty and intuition; Schwartz continues: "I believe most of us know in our hearts, when we are uncomfortable in our skins or unhappy in our jobs or when we do not feel sheltered in our own homes. We know when a relationship isn't working or a friendship has run its course. But we are often reluctant to own up to what we

89

know, even to ourselves, because then we might have to do something about it. Inertia is a powerful force. We have heard the rationale about the devil you know being preferable to the one you don't; many of us choose the path of least resistance—*even as our inner voice encourages us to deviate from it*" (bold italics mine).

How true! And she brings her confessional thought piece and my creative insight to fitting closure with a personal anecdote of going to a restaurant with friends *that her inner voice had told her not to go to*: "But as I left the restaurant, I thought how an evening that should have been pleasant had left me feeling wrung out and blue. I thought how I wished I had chosen to listen to my own voice, to be truer to myself. Why hadn't I simply bowed out of dinner? I thought how I had spent too long in this life pretending that things were fine when they weren't—and that I liked things when I didn't: things like soul-crushing meals in restaurants. And asparagus."

I put the paper down, smiling once more at the miraculous power of synchronicity; and then I called the archetypal lady seeker back up from the depths of my creative unconscious and shared Susan Schwartz's soul-scouring article with her.

The lady seeker smiled, and contritely responded: "She's right. I don't hear my little voice, because I only hear what I want to hear. So, tell me more about this teaching."

"That," I said, "would be another scenario."

———————

The archetypal lady seeker in my imaginary scenario heard the call with the accidental drowning of her young daughter and went on a spiritual quest; but she couldn't make up her mind which path to follow because she had been conditioned by life to be distrustful.

Ironically, her distrust of life led her to be doubtful of her inner self's guidance; that's why she couldn't make up her mind which path to follow. This was my quandary when I was on my spiritual quest for my true self. I was plagued by the question: *how can I be sure that I'm making the right decision?*

I know now that in the Divine Plan of God there are no wrong decisions, because every path we take leads back home to God; but some paths are harder to walk than others, and we don't know which will one will be harder. So we're right back to where we started: *how can we be sure that we're making the right decision?*

I was haunted by this question, to the point of decision-paralysis at times; so I had to find a solution. That's when the idea struck me to do something as bold, if not bolder, than my decision to live my *Royal Dictum*: I decided to let go and let God.

If I couldn't trust myself to make the right decision, I would let God decide for me; but how? How could I be absolutely certain that God would decide for me?

I WOULD FLIP A COIN! Heads, I do; tails, I don't. And that's how I made up my mind for the more difficult decisions of my life—like asking a woman I liked out on a date, for example. But letting go and letting God only worked if I was true to the flip. If I wasn't true to the flip, I would be cheating God and myself; so I had to do what the coin decided.

For about six months I was true to the flip, making every big decision by letting go and letting God decide for me; but then I began to notice a very strange phenomenon. I began to notice that God's decisions perfectly coincided with how I felt.

I honestly doubt that anyone will believe me, but I began to notice that how I felt about what I should do was validated by the flip of my coin. If I strongly felt that I should do something and asked God to decide for me with a flip of the coin, the coin always agreed with me; and if I strongly felt that I shouldn't do something, the coin agreed with me.

I continued to observe this strange phenomenon until I finally connected the dots and realized that I no longer needed God to make up my mind for me!

By daring to let go and let God decide for me, I learned to hone my decision-making instincts; and I came to the startling realization that *my will and God's will were in perfect accord as long as I trusted myself!*

And I stopped my bold experiment with a healthy new respect for the advice that Polonius gave to his son Laertes who was about to catch a boat to Paris in Shakespeare's play *Hamlet*: This above all: to thine own self be true, /And it must follow, as the night the day, /Thou canst not then be false to any man." ***Because the more true we are to*** *ourselves, the more we can be sure that we're on the right path to God!*

29. Socrates' Secret

"I" is the big mystery of life. "I" is a miraculous unit of reflective self-consciousness that is aware of its own individuality and separateness from life; and although every "I" is made of the same individuated consciousness of life, each "I", in the words of the Romantic poet John Keats, "possesses a bliss peculiar to each one by individual existence." "I" is who we are. It is our distinct individual *core identity*. Like snowflakes, we are all different but the same; but how do we become different? Better still, how do we even become a distinct, separate "I"?

Gurdjieff believed that we do not have a *core identity* that we call "I". According to Gurdjieff, we are only born with the potential to create our own immortal soul; and the essential purpose of his teaching had to do with creating this *core identity* we call "I".

"Man has no individuality," said Gurdjieff, in one of his talks to his inner circle of students. "He has no single, big I. Man is divided into a multiplicity of small I's. And each separate small I is able to call itself by the name of the Whole, to act in the name of the Whole, to agree or disagree, to give promises, to make decisions with which another I or the Whole will have to deal. This explains why people so often make decisions and so seldom carry them out…" (P. D. Ouspensky, *In Search of the Miraculous*, p. 60).

In effect, Gurdjieff taught how to fuse the many fragmented little I's into one big I, which would be one's *core identity* and immortal soul. This is the promise of his teaching, and although he was wrong about man's soul, I know that Gurdjieff's teaching works.

Gurdjieff attracted me because I saw in his teaching a way to find my true self. I went on my quest for my true self because of what I did that infamous night that shocked my conscience awake, so I resonated with the concept that one separate little I can do something that the Whole will be responsible for; that's why I dove into his teaching.

It didn't matter to me then if Gurdjieff was right or wrong about man's soul; all that mattered was finding my true self. I didn't know then that I had a *core identity* in my Soul self; but as I lived Gurdjieff's teaching I fused my many separate little I's into one "Work I" that brought me closer to my Soul self, and along with my *Royal Dictum* and sayings of Jesus I transformed the consciousness of my "Work I" and coincided with my Soul self. That's how I resolved the paradoxical conundrum of Gurdjieff's teaching.

Socrates knew that we have an immortal soul, which he believed was trapped in the prison of our mortal body. "There is a doctrine uttered in secret that man is a prisoner who has no right to open the door of his prison and run away," he says in Plato's *Phaedo*. "This is a great mystery which I do not quite understand," he adds; but the key word is "quite," because it implies that he does understand the mystery, but not to his satisfaction.

There is no end to the mystery of Soul, so with characteristic modesty Socrates was being truthful; but he understood the mystery enough to provide us with a key that opens the door to man's prison. "For I deem that the true disciple of philosophy is likely to be misunderstood by other men," he says in the *Phaedo*; "they do not perceive that he is ever pursuing death and dying; and if this is true, why, having had the desire of death all his life, should he repine at the arrival of that which he has been always pursuing and desiring?"

The *Phaedo* is Plato's account of Socrates' final discourse before he takes his life by drinking hemlock. "Do we believe that there is such a thing as death?" he asks.

"To be sure," replied Simmias.

"And is this anything but the separation of the soul and body?" replied Socrates. "And being dead is the attainment of this separation; when the soul exists in herself, and is parted from the body and the body is parted from the soul—that is death?"

"Exactly; that and nothing else," replied Simmias.

The death that the true disciple of philosophy is pursuing is the metaphorical death of the ephemeral, ego self ("dying before dying," as the Sufis say); because ego obfuscates man's perception of his Soul self. In effect, Socrates is saying that ego is our prison; and to open the door of our prison we have to transform our ego self. And according to Socrates we can do this by living a life of virtue, of which he held Goodness to be the most noble; which is why I made *doing good* the ethical principle of my life.

A life of virtue purifies the ego, and as the ego is purified by the transformative power of virtue we die the metaphorical death of separating soul from the body. "And what is purification but the separation of soul from the body, as I was saying before; the habit of soul gathering and collecting herself into herself, out of all the courses of the body; and dwelling in her own place alone, as in another life, so also in this, as far as she can; the release of the soul from the chains of the body," said Socrates in the *Phaedo*.

Socrates reveals something here that took me years to recognize. He does not spell it out, but it is implied in his comment *"the habit of soul gathering and collecting herself into herself."* After years of living the Way *consciously*, it finally dawned upon me that ***the "I" of our Soul self and the "I" of our ego self is one and the same "I",*** and "the habit of soul gathering and collecting herself into herself" was merely Socrates's way of saying that we are one immortal Soul self that splits in two when we are reborn into life. And this means that contrary to the Buddhist belief, ***ego is our Soul self not-yet-realized; and it is REAL.***

This is what Jesus meant by the two becoming one. In the *Gospel of Thomas* Jesus was asked by someone when the kingdom of heaven would come, and he replied: **"When the two will be as one, and the outer like the inner, and the male with the female, neither male nor female."** (*The Unknown Sayings of Jesus*, Marvin Meyer, p. 95)

"Kingdom of heaven" was Christ's metaphor for **both** the Way **and** the eternal life of Soul; and as I "worked" on myself with Gurdjieff's teaching, my *Royal Dictum*, Christ's sayings, and a host of inherently self-transcending principles that I garnered from all walks of life, I made the two into one and one fine summer day gave birth to my spiritual self in my mother's kitchen while she was kneading bread dough. That's why I could write in my journal: *I am what I am not, and I am not what I am; I am both, but neither: I am Soul.*

When I shared this with Carl Jung in my dream, his eyes twinkled with delight, and I knew that it no longer bothered him that I had managed to "pull it off."

30. The Meaningless Life

Our greatest need in life is to be our true self; but to be who we are we have to *become* who we are. This sounds nonsensical, but it's not. The acorn seed's greatest need—*nay, it's only need!*—is to become an oak tree. The same with any seed in life; it is teleologically driven to become what it is genetically encoded to be, and so with man.

My greatest need in life was to find my true self, and in my efforts to satisfy my greatest need I learned that to find my true self I had to *become* my true self. It took a lot of time, wisdom, courage, and perseverance; but happily, I did experience that moment of self-coincidence when my two selves became one.

In the famous BBC Face to Face interview with Carl Gustav Jung, John Freeman asked Jung his closing question, and Jung's answer brought tears to my eyes because he verified what I've come to realize about the individuating self of man:

FREEMAN: *As the world becomes more technically efficient it seems increasingly necessary for people to behave communally and collectively. Now, do you think it possible that the higher development of man may be to submerge his own individuality in a kind of collective consciousness?*

JUNG: That's hardly possible. I think there will be a reaction. A reaction will set in against this communal dissociation. You know, man doesn't stand for ever his nullification. Once there will be a reaction, and I see it setting in. You know, *when I think of my patients, they all seek their own existence and to assure their existence against the complete atomization into nothingness, or into meaninglessness. Man cannot stand a meaningless life* (bold italics mine).

If man's greatest need in life is to *become* who he is meant to be, which Jung verified and I happily confirmed with my own quest for my true self, why would the Buddhist tradition continue to maintain the counterintuitive concept of the non-existence of the self?

"The essence of the Buddhist practice is therefore to get rid of that illusion of a self which so falsifies our view of the world," said the Tibetan monk Matthieu Ricard in *The Monk and the Philosopher*. This perspective so offended my sense of reality that I had to respond to it in my book *Stupidity Is Not a Gift of God* with a personal essay on the evolutionary impulse to individuate. But I would not have responded had I not experienced what I did when I had my fourth past-life regression, which gave me personal proof of the individuation process of life that was set into motion with my experience of the inception of life on Planet Earth when my I-consciousness *animated* the amino acids (the first building blocks of life) that were created out of the blended gasses from the earth and sky.

My incredible fourth past-life regression was testimony to the Divine Plan of God, and as much as I would love to play my hand now, I cannot; the dialectic of this essay demands a more satisfying context for my hand to be shown. Credibility is at stake, and I don't want to be accused of some kind of philosophical *legerdemain*.

But I can ask the question now: if we don't have an immortal soul (a *core self*), why do we recall our past lives in our dreams and under hypnotic regression?

I've read many books on past-life regression—Dr. Brian L. Weiss, Dr. Michael Newton, Dolores Cannon, and psychic Sylvia Fraser to name only a select few—and not once in the thousands and thousands of past-life regressions that they conducted did their clients fail to be regressed to a past life. Not one person came up blank. They may not have succeeded in the first regression, or second even; but eventually they were brought back to a past lifetime. So, what's the explanation for this mysterious phenomenon?

Either they all had past lives, or they tapped into that pool of "soul soup" and recalled an archetypal matrix of energy that identified itself with individuality—a "particular stream of consciousness," as Tibetan monk Matthieu Ricard declared. "That the self has no true existence doesn't prevent one particular stream of consciousness from having qualities that distinguish it from another stream," he says in *The Monk and the Philosopher*.

In a book edited by Michael Newton, Ph.D., *Memories of the Afterlife, Life between Lives* ("stories of personal transformation"), there are many case studies of individual souls that were regressed to their life between life; and we learn from these case studies that these souls discussed whether they had accomplished what they had "contracted" to accomplish in the life they had just lived. In effect, they went into their new life with a karmic obligation *(sacred contract)* to fulfill, and if they did fulfill it they could continue on their journey to "wholeness and singleness of self" with less karmic baggage.

All the evidence points to soul's natural impulse to individuate into "wholeness and singleness of self," which is the purpose of a soul's evolution through the *exoteric* first circle of life; but when the natural process of karmic evolution can no longer satisfy a soul's longing to be, then one begins to suffer the *unbearable longing* to be one's true self—as I did, as Carl Jung did, and as the artist Jerry Wennstrom did.

Jerry Wennstrom tells his incredible story in his book *The Inspired Heart* of how his personal path of art had brought him as far as it possible could, and he abandoned his art and "let go and let God" to satisfy his *unbearable longing* to be his true self.

"In 1979, I destroyed all the art I had created, gave everything I owned away, and began a new life...I trusted a higher good that I sensed was much better equipped to inform my choices than anything I had available in the limited range of will and intelligence," he writes in his introduction to *The Inspired Heart.*

And for fifteen years Jerry Wennstrom lived a life of unconditional trust in God, or "the Universe" as he preferred to call the omniscient guiding force of his life; and when he had satisfied his *unbearable longing* enough to step back into the mainstream of life, he took up art again—but from a totally new perspective now, which he confirmed: "I hold true that the path lived attentively is a sacred path, and that the fundamental spirit of art is alive, well, and deeply esoteric. As does any spiritual path, art has the potential to deliver us into our own true *becoming*, which is identical to our world's becoming. Art expresses and defines the deep and collective spirit of our time."

But to realize this, Jerry Wennstrom had to reconnect with his "inner artist", which was why he dared to go on his own hero's journey by letting go of his old life ("dying before dying") and letting God govern his new life, proving yet again that *life is an individual journey*…

31. Gauguin's Famous Three Questions

If literature is not enough, as Katherine Mansfield came to realize, and if art is not enough, as Jerry Wennstrom came to realize, does this not imply that literature and art could no longer satisfy their inner longing to be?

If our greatest need in life is to be who we are, as the acorn seed's greatest need is to be an oak tree and not a monkey, *what is it that we crave to be?* This was the second question of the artist Paul Gauguin's famous painting, which he titled: "Where Do We Come From? What Are We? Where Are We Going?

In the game of poker, a royal flush is the best hand possible; and the answer to these three questions would be equal to a royal flush in the game of life. But what are the odds of getting a royal flush? Very high; but not impossible.

Life is like a game of poker. We play the hand that we are dealt and hope that one day we will get a royal flush. And if we play long enough, that day will come; because the odds, as high as they are, will have to favor us eventually. This is why Paul Twitchell said, "If you don't get it right in this life, you will just keep coming back until you do."

I came back again and again, and each time I came back I played the hand that I had dealt myself by my own karmic obligations, and I didn't much care for some of the hands that I had to play out—like my insufferable lifetime as Solomon, the Good slave; or my infamous lifetime as *"le salaud de Paris"*; or my delusional lifetime as Salaam, the Sufi.

But I had no choice. I created the karma responsible for each of these lives, and I had to play each hand out to fulfill my *sacred contract.* And then I was born into the aristocracy of London, England in my former life to set the stage for my current lifetime where I made a *sacred contract* to get it right this time.

I loathed the hypocrisy of the aristocracy; but without realizing it I became what I most despised about human nature, and I fled from the "foul beast of honor and deceit" and lived out the rest of my life as a trapper in the new land of the Americas.

For eight years I worked indefatigably just to survive, but as I worked I reflected on my own hypocrisy; and just as I was about to break the code of Christ's paradoxical sayings (the one that I centered on was the most agonizing: *"He that loveth his life shall lose it; and he that hateth his life in this world shall keep it unto life eternal"* John 12: 24), a black bear cut my life short by swatting me on the side of the head and knocking me into the river where I left my body with the greatest feeling of relief I had ever experienced.

I set the stage for my current life in my former aristocratic-trapper lifetime, because I confronted my own hypocrisy and began the transformation of my life by "dying before dying." I vowed to "dismantle my false (aristocratic) personality and rebuild myself," but unfortunately my life was cut short; and I vowed on the other side that in my next life I would complete what I had vowed to do in my aristocratic-trapper life—*which was to satisfy the unbearable longing in my soul to be my true self!*

I compromised my soul in my aristocratic lifetime by forfeiting it to the "foul beast of honor and deceit" for the sweet pleasures of my formidable wit; but I was fortunate enough to become aware of what I had done, and I vowed to reclaim my lost soul. I fled London and sailed to the new land of the Americas to become a penitent trapper; and I came into my current lifetime to complete what I had failed to accomplish in my former life.

But I hit a snag in my current life. I did not satisfy that *unbearable longing* in my soul, and I died to my current life with a desperate feeling of regret that I had not lived the life that I was meant to live; that's why, as I was informed by Ascended Master St. Padre Pio, I chose to be reborn into my same life again to achieve a different outcome. And in this, my parallel life, I have fulfilled the obligation of my *sacred contract* to find my lost soul; and I *know* that when I leave this lifetime I will have no regrets.

32. What Is Our Sacred Contract?

Getting it right. This was the *sacred contract* that I came to fulfill in my current parallel life. I feel foolish talking about my parallel life, because it sounds much too far-fetched that I would reincarnate into the body of a life that I have already lived once; but, as Jesus said in Glenda Green's book *Love without End, Jesus Speaks:*

"Your immortality is not imprisoned within a wheel of life, or pathways of cause and effect. Neither are you the product of linear evolvement. You were created in perfection, and perfect love, and you do continue to re-manifest infinitely, but it is according to the will of the Father, and according to your own purposes, your own love, and your own place of service and learning."

Jesus has opened the door here for me to offer my understanding of the Divine Plan of God as I discerned it when I connected the missing pieces that I was privileged to receive when I had my seven past-life regressions; and the simplest explanation of the DPG (Divine Plan of God) is that **we have two destinies: one spiritual, and one karmic.**

Jesus refers to our spiritual destiny as "the will of our Father," and our karmic destiny as our personal destiny "according to your own purposes, your own love, and your own place of service and learning." Our spiritual destiny is divinely pre-scripted ("the will of the Father); and our karmic destiny is scripted according to our own will. And by **"getting it right"** Paul Twitchell meant that we have to align our personal karmic destiny with our pre-scripted spiritual destiny, which was my *sacred contract* in my current parallel life.

How, then, did I manage to "pull it off," as Jung so impishly put it?

Because life is an individual journey, each soul will have their own unique point of entry into the mysteries of the Way; or, if you will, each soul will be initiated into the *mesoteric* circle of life according to their own individual karmic makeup. Like Jung, Jerry Wennstrom, and myself for example.

As Jung said in *The Red Book*, "This life is the way, the long sought-after way to the unfathomable, which we call divine." But because no two people have the same karma, no two paths in life will be the same. That's why the Sufis say that there are as many paths to God as there are souls of man, and why Jung was so fond of quipping (with an impish twinkle in his eye, no doubt), "Thank God I'm Jung and not a Jungian."

But what does it mean to say that our own life is the path, "the long sought-after way to the unfathomable, which we call divine"?

As I came to understand the DPG, it means that we have to align our karmic destiny with our spiritual destiny. We create the circumstances of our personal karmic destiny by the choices we make, but our spiritual destiny is pre-scripted; and our two destinies have to be aligned to achieve "wholeness and singleness of self."

The Greek poet Cleanthes captured man's conundrum in his stoic poem, "Hymn to Zeus"— *Lead me, O Zeus, and thou Destiny/ the way I am bid by thee to go./ To follow I am willing;/ for were I recusant, I do but make myself a slave/ and still must follow.*

We are all sparks of God teleologically driven to realize our spiritual nature. That's what Jesus referred to as "the will of the Father." But because we have free will, we create our own karmic destiny from one life to the next, which can be at variance with "the will of the Father." Getting it right then would be learning how to align our karmic destiny with our spiritual destiny; and the only way to do that is to live a life that is not at variance with "the will of the Father." And herein lies our problem, because who's to say what God's will is?

This was my conundrum, which I finally managed to resolve with my unbelievably bold experiment of "letting go and letting God." The artist Jerry Wennstrom did the same when he hit his own brick wall, only in accordance with his own karmic makeup. I tossed a coin to let God decided for me, and Jerry simply watched and listened for guidance from the "Universe," and as he tells us in *The Inspired Heart* he experienced some amazing synchronicities on his personal path to "wholeness and singleness of self."

OREST STOCCO

The Way is the Way is the Way, but it is always an individual path; and it leads, guides, and instructs us on our personal path with signs, symbols, coincidences both small and large, dreams, waking dreams, and any way possible that will get our attention for the sole purpose of helping us align our karmic destiny with our spiritual destiny.

33. Jung and Reincarnation

Just how then did I "get it right"? What was it about my personal path that bothered Jung enough to ask me how I had managed to "pull it off"?

Jung read my book *The Way of Soul* with no less attention than he paid to his ancient Gnostic and Alchemy texts when he was hot on the trail of the Way, because he intuited the Way in my personal path; but for some reason he couldn't put his finger on just how I had managed to solve the riddle that had taken him the better part of the second half of his life to figure out; and still, the mystery continued to haunt him until I showed my hand.

Jung didn't believe in reincarnation. Not until late in life, anyway. He never came right out and admitted it, because he was compelled to preserve the scientific integrity of his psychology; but he came as close as he possibly could to admitting his belief in *Memories, Dreams, Reflections*: "I could well imagine that I have lived in former centuries and there encountered questions I was not yet able to answer; that I had to be born again because I had not fulfilled that task that was given to me. When I die, my deeds will follow along with me—that is how I imagine it. I will bring with me what I have done…" (p. 318).

That was Jung's karmic destiny, to "fulfill that task that was given to me." What his task was specifically, no one knows for sure (maybe he didn't know himself); but in my dream he began by saying that the central mystery of his life was "the alpha and omega of the self," and even on the other side he was still plagued by that mystery.

What is the self? Where does it come from? Where is it going? These are the questions that Jung sought to answer with *daemonic* dedication; and he sums up his life's research on the question of the self in *Memories, Dreams, Reflections*:

"Unconscious wholeness therefore seems to be the true *spiritus rector* of all biological and psychic events. Here is a principle which strives for total realization—which in man's case signifies the

OREST STOCCO

attainment of total consciousness. Attainment of consciousness is culture in the broadest sense, and self-knowledge is therefore the heart and essence of this process. The Oriental attributes unquestionably divine significance to the self, and according to ancient Christian (Gnostic) view self-knowledge is the road to knowledge of God. The decisive question for man is: *Is he related to something infinite or not? That is the telling question of his life*" (pp. 324-5, italics mine).

Jung answered this "telling question" on the BBC Face to Face interview when John Freeman took him by surprise with the question, "Do you now believe in God."

Jung paused, and by the look in his eyes we can see that he feels he has been tricked by the clever interviewer; but Jung has too much integrity to duck the question, even though he knows that his answer is going to bedevil him down the road (which it did, because it gave his critics what they needed to label him a "Gnostic" and "mystic").

"Difficult to answer," Jung replied. "I know. I don't need to believe. I know."

This is pure Gnosticism, because the Gnostic *knows* through experience; and after one reads Jung's *Red Book* one can understand why he would answer this way; but it was enough to send shock waves throughout the scientific community, and Jung had to write an open letter to "The Listener" (July 26, 1960) to explain what he meant.

Despite his explanation, however, Jung confessed his true feelings in his answer to John Freeman's surprise question—which he admitted to me in my dream when I asked him why he tried to duck his answer in his open letter to the newspaper.

I was as devilish with him as he was with me, and he broke into laughter and came clean; and this paved the way for the most remarkable conversation that I have ever had on the secret teachings of *The Way of Soul* with a man who was as intimately familiar with his own path to "wholeness and singleness of self" as I was with mine...

106

34. The Man with No Centre

When all is said and done, "getting it right" comes down to creating the *right kind of personality*; one that is inherently self-transcending.

Although this is what I was striving to accomplish as I lived my personal path that I had forged in "the smithy of my soul" (to borrow a phrase from Joyce's *A Portrait of the Artist as a Young Man*) out of Gurdjieff's teaching, my *Royal Dictum*, the sayings of Jesus, and dozens of wisdom sayings that I garnered from all walks of life, I did not suddenly come to the realization that creating the *right kind of personality* was the essential purpose of all spiritual paths in the world; I grew into this realization slowly.

But as I sadly came to learn, one can be a good Christian, a good Buddhist, a good Muslim, a good Theosophist or whatever and still not transcend the dual consciousness of their nature—the *being* and *non-being* aspect of their Soul self; that's what "getting it right" is all about. Unless one creates a personality that is inherently self-transcending and resolves the dual consciousness of their Soul self, they will remain trapped in the Mental Plane of Consciousness—like the great spiritual teacher Krishnamurti, for example.

I could never explain my uneasy feelings for Krishnamurti. I read him because he was touted to be a great spiritual teacher who had influenced Allan Watts, Aldous Huxley, and a whole host of spiritual seekers; but I could never get a fix on him. And the harder I tried to pin him down, the more frustrated I became—like trying to read Joyce's *Finnegan's Wake*.

I love the early James Joyce and often go back to *The Dubliners*, his book of short stories; and I drew a great deal of inspiration in high school from his autobiographical novel *A Portrait of the Artist as a Young Man*; but he began to get pedantic and abstruse with *Ulysses*, considered to be the best novel ever written, and impenetrably recondite with his final novel *Finnegan's Wake*. With Krishnamurti, I met him at his most spiritually obscure; and despite how brilliant he seemed to be, I could never find my way in his teaching. And I moved on, as I always did whenever a path could not satisfy my *need to know*.

I never understood my instinctive antipathy for Krishnamurti, but one day many years later when I was doing research online for a book I was writing, I came across Laura Huxley's recollection of meeting Krishnamurti in Zurich, Switzerland.

Laura was Aldous Huxley's second wife, and she and Aldous and Krishnamurti were having luncheon at the home of yoga master Vanda Scaravelli. After what Laura described as a delicious but completely vegetarian luncheon, Aldous and Signora S. left her and Krishnamurti to have a private conversation; and during this very private talk I learned what it was about Krishnamurti that made me so uneasy.

Over luncheon, they talked about food recipes, which led into Laura's book *Recipes for Living and Loving*, which she was still working on; but Krishnamurti was too polite to tell her what he really thought of her book. In private however he spoke his mind: "You know, I think that those people who go about helping other people...those people, they are a curse!" This, of course, implied Laura and her recipe book for living and loving.

This perplexed Laura Huxley, and she replied that that's what he did with his talks; but he responded by saying, "But I don't do it on purpose."

Puzzled, she asked him to explain; and he replied that he was not a healer, a psychologist, a therapist or any of those things; he was only a religious man, and "alcoholics or neurotics or addicts—it doesn't matter what the trouble is—they get better quite often—but that is not important; that is not the point—that is only the consequence."

"What is wrong with such a consequence? I only give people techniques or recipes or tools to help them to do what they need to do—what is wrong in using the transformation of energy to change those miserable feelings into constructive behavior?"

"No! No!" exploded Krishnamurti. "Techniques. Transformation-no-rubbish! One must destroy-destroy...everything!"

Flabbergasted, Laura said: "But what do you do?"

"Nothing. I am only a religious man."

DO WE HAVE AN IMMORTAL SOUL?

Still unable to get a fix on Krishnamurti, she asked, "What is a religious man?"

"Krishnamurti changed his tone and rhythm," wrote Laura Huxley in her memoir *This Timeless Moment.* "He spoke now calmly, with incisiveness. 'I will tell you what a religious man is. First of all, a religious man is a man who is alone—not lonely, you understand, but alone—with no theories or dogmas, no opinion, no background. He is alone and loves it—free of conditioning and alone—and enjoying it. Second, a religious man must be both man and woman—I don't mean sexually—but he must know the dual nature of everything; a religious man must feel and be both masculine and feminine. Third,' and now his manner intensified again, 'to be a religious man, one must destroy everything—destroy the past, destroy one's convictions, interpretations, deceptions—destroy all self-hypnosis—destroy until there is no center; you understand, no center.'"

No center? After a silence, Krishnamurti said quietly, "Then you are a religious person. Then stillness comes. Completely still."

There it was, the reason why I had an instinctive repulsion for Krishnamurti—because his teaching would have pulled me into the great vortex of NOTHINGNESS from which I had devoted my whole life to liberating myself from!

Noman has no center, and not until one resolves the consciousness of his *being* and *non-being* and becomes both but neither will they realize their transcendent Soul self—which was precisely why I had such an instinctive aversion for Krishnamurti and natural attraction to Carl Gustav Jung and his psychology of individuation…

35. My Solar Cult Experience

"Memoir is the facts of life. Fiction is the truth of life," said our own Canadian Nobel laureate Alice Munroe. Well, my experience with an offshoot Christian solar cult teaching would best be told in a work of fiction (which I may have the courage to write one day), but I feel compelled to mention it here because it will help explain to what extremes one will go to satisfy their *unbearable longing* for "wholeness and singleness of self."

I shared my traumatizing experience with Jung in my dream, and he understood why I would do such a foolish thing; because, as he reveals in *Memories, Dreams, Reflections,* "There was a *daemon* in me, and in the end its presence proved decisive. It overpowered me, and if I was at times ruthless it was because I was in the grips of the *daemon*. I could never stop at anything once attained. I had to hasten on, to catch up to my vision" (p. 356).

So driven was I by the vision of my own *daemon* that my father once described me to my cousin's husband, who had just come over from Italy, as someone who would go to hell to get what he needed; that's how single-minded I had become in my quest for my true self. But this time I paid a very dear price: I did irreparable damage to my eyesight.

"Spirituality cannot be taught, it must be caught," said Paul Twitchell; and that's what I learned to do with Gurdjieff's teaching, my *Royal Dictum*, and the sayings of Jesus. So good did I become at "catching" the spiritual energy of life that I gave birth to my spiritual self in my mother's kitchen one day while she was kneading bread dough on the kitchen table; but like a newborn infant child that has to have its mother's milk to survive, so too did I *crave* spiritual energy to nourish my newborn spiritual self.

That's how I fell for that offshoot Christian solar cult teaching that promised this spiritual energy (which it called the Logos) that was allegedly imbued with the rays of the sun which one ingested by practicing secret "solar techniques"—a very DANGEROUS and foolish thing to do, but which I did nonetheless and irreparably damaged my eyes.

I practiced these "solar techniques" for a little over three years before I began to feel a burning sensation in my eyes that I had to have checked out. When the ophthalmologist asked me how I got the three burns in my eyes, I foolishly told him; and he got so angry with me that he stormed out of the examination room and refused to treat me.

I had to fly to the eye clinic in Waterloo, Ontario for the appointment that my older brother very kindly set up for me with expeditious efficiency, and there I learned that the solar burns were stationary and not degenerative; and I cannot describe how relieved I was when I heard this, because for one whole week I suffered the unbearable dread of going blind because that's what I was led to believe by the ill-tempered ophthalmologist who called me crazy and refused to treat me.

I can see well enough today, but the three pinhole solar burns in the retina of my eyes, two in my right eye and one in my left, make reading very taxing. My impaired vision strains me to the point of fatigue; not physical fatigue, but a kind of mental fatigue that makes me want to close my eyes and rest throughout the course of the day.

Because I studied this teaching by correspondence, I never met the explorer/seeker who brought this ancient secret teaching out into the world; but in my third year I began to smell something rotten in the state of Denmark, so I flew to Reno, Nevada for a workshop; but the moment I shook this man's hand I felt the strangest sensation: with what seemed like a silent swoosh, I felt his energy field instantly sucked into his body, and the look in his eyes told me everything that I needed to know; and that same day I dropped the teaching.

But the damage had already been done. Shortly after I returned from Reno, I began to feel a burning sensation in my eyes; and thus began the most humiliating experience of my entire life as I tried to explain myself to my eye doctors, and my family.

This experience happened more than thirty years ago, but I still don't have enough courage to write about it; and it was *shadow-affected* experiences like this that inspired my book *Stupidity Is Not a Gift of God*. I did start a novel ten or twelve years ago called *The Sunworshipper*, but I can't bring myself to finish it. Maybe one day I will, just to show how possessed one can become when he's caught in the grip of his *daemonic* spirit.

36. The Acorn Theory

"Your daemon is the carrier of your destiny," says Jungian analyst James Hillman in his book *The Soul's Code, In Search of Character and Calling.* Although Hillman does not advance reincarnation in his personal version of Jungian psychotherapy, it is certainly implied when he writes: "As explained by the greatest of later Platonists, Plotinus (A. D. 205-270), we elected the body, the parents, the place, and the circumstances that suited the soul and that, as the myth says, belongs to its necessity. This suggests that the circumstances, including my body and my parents whom I may curse, are my soul's own choice—and I do not understand this because I have forgotten" (*The Soul's Code*, p. 8).

Hillman says that his book is about "calling, about fate, about character, about innate image. Together they make up the 'acorn theory,' which holds that each person bears a uniqueness that asks to be lived and that is already present before it is lived" (*The Soul's Code*, p. 6); but this is precisely what our *karmic destiny* is all about.

As the acorn seed is called to become an oak tree, so are we called by our own *karmic destiny* to be who we are meant to be; this, essentially, is what Hillman means by his *acorn theory.* He writes: "The acorn theory proposes that you and I and every single person is born with a defining image. Individuality resides in a formal cause— to use old philosophical language going back to Aristotle. We each embody our own idea, in the language of Plato and Plotinus. And this form, this idea, this image does not tolerate too much straying. The theory also attributes to this innate image an angelic or *daemonic* intention, as if it were a spark of consciousness; and, moreover, holds that it has our interest at heart because it chose us for its reasons" (*The Soul's Code,* pp. 11-12).

This is precisely what happened to the poet David Whyte, whose book *Crossing the Unknown Sea, Work as a Pilgrimage of Identity* introduces the reader to the Way in the work that we do—if we but adopt the right attitude towards our work (*"a firm persuasion,"* says Whyte); which only goes to prove what every seeker will one day realize, that the Way is everywhere to be found because it is the omnipresent, omniscient guiding force of life. But David Whyte did not realize this until he was called by his personal *daemon* to drop what he was doing and take up his path of writing poetry.

His is a fascinating story, full of amazing synchronicities (as is the story of every person that has been called by their *karmic destiny*); but David Whyte did not take up his calling to poetry early in life as the more undaunted poets do, despite the clarion call that he heard as a young boy: "I remember the absolute sense of excitement at nine years old, when I picked up my first book of poetry and read it as if I had discovered a secret code of my future life—which, as it turned out, I had." (*Crossing the Unknown Sea*, p. 64).

The better, or more seasoned judgment of the adult world around him persuaded David to take up a safe career that would earn him a living; and he graduated with a degree in Marine Zoology and landed a formative position as a naturalist guide in the Galapagos Islands, where he lived and worked for ten years before moving to the Pacific Northwest of the United States to work for a non-profit institute; but when he had a been "cooked" enough by life (as the Sufis like to say about how life makes one ready for their *karmic destiny*), David heard the call so loud and clear one day at work that he was forced by the sheer imperative of his *unbearable longing* to drop what he was doing and take up the path that he had been called to embark upon in his youth—*writing poetry*.

David Whyte gave himself to his professional work so thoroughly that he literally lost himself to himself. He writes in his memoir: "One morning, hurtling from my desk toward the photocopier, I passed a roomful of my colleagues just about to start a meeting. There was someone I needed to talk to. I saw immediately that he wasn't among them, but I put my head in the door before they could begin, and in a very loud, urgent voice, I said, 'Has anyone seen David?'" (*Crossing the Unknown Sea,* p. 124).

There was a moment of stunned silence, and then spontaneous laughter at the realization that David was totally serious but absolutely oblivious to the fact that he was the only person who worked there called David. That's how far he had strayed from his *karmic destiny*. "I was looking for David, all right, and I couldn't find him," he writes. "In fact, I hadn't seen him for a very long time. I was looking for a David who had disappeared under a swampy morass of stress and speed. In the humiliation of that moment, caught forever in a doorway, calling my own name, I saw that I had become a stranger to myself" (p. 125).

Not unlike Jung who had lost his soul on his way to realizing everything he had ever wished for, "honor, power, wealth, knowledge, and every human happiness," so too did David Whyte lose himself in the pursuits of his work; and if asking his colleagues if they had seen David wasn't the *Trickster* trying to get his attention, then I don't know what the *Trickster effect* is; and David Whyte, like Carl Jung and Jerry Wennstrom, whom Whyte got to know personally and admire, began his own hero's journey by risking economic security and taking the road less travelled—just as the poet Robert Frost had done!

Today his life as a poet has created a loyal readership and listenership in three areas: the literate world of reading that most poets inhabit, the psychological and theological worlds of philosophical enquiry, and the world of vocation, work, and organizational leadership. David Whyte is on course to "wholeness and singleness of self."

37. The Great Slayer of the Real

"The acorn theory holds that each person bears a uniqueness that asks to be lived and that is already present before it is lived," says James Hillman. I agree completely; only I would add that our uniqueness is born of our own individual karma.

We may all be sparks of consciousness that come from God, but Mother Nature is responsible for the natural individuation of our Soul self in the *exoteric* first circle of life. From one life to the next, we *become* our Soul self as we create and resolve the karma that we create with each choice we make. This is the cycle of life and death, the *being* and *non-being* aspect of our nature that Socrates referred to as our prison; and we will never escape from the endless cycle of life and death until we find the key to our prison door. *But we will never look for the key to our prison door until we realize that we are in prison!*

I was awakened to my own prison when I was compelled by my *archetypal shadow self* to have a sexual experience that brutally shocked my conscience awake, and I vowed to find a way out of the prison of my own nature. I knew that the person who did what he did that night was me, but I also knew that it was not the real me; and I went on a quest to find my true self (just as I had done in my former aristocratic-trapper life). So did Carl Jung, Jerry Wennstrom, and David Whyte; and the only difference between us was the unique nature of our own individual *karmic destiny*.

Jung was a psychologist, Wennstrom an artist, Whyte a marine biologist and nascent poet, and I was a housepainter/seeker who aspired to be a writer; and we all came to that point in our life where we simply had to satisfy that *unbearable longing* in our soul for "wholeness and singleness of self." In a word, we craved to be our true self; and to do that we had to, in the words of Gary Zukav (*The Seat of the Soul*), "align our personality with our soul." This was our *karmic destiny...*

DO WE HAVE AN IMMORTAL SOUL?

The karma that we create today is responsible for the life we live tomorrow, and the karma that we create in our current lifetime will determine the unique character of our next life; this is the natural individuation process of our Soul self, and the reason that the Buddhist concept of the *non-self* so offends my sense of reality.

I *knew* that it was me when I experienced myself in another body in another time in my past-life recollection dreams, and I *knew* that it was me in another body in another time when I had my seven past-life regressions; but the question that I spent the best part of my life trying to answer was this: *who was the "me" that I experienced in those other lifetimes?*

According to the ancient doctrine of reincarnation that Socrates alludes to in Plato's Dialogues, it was my immortal soul; but the Buddhist perspective considers this "me" to be non-existent. It is merely a "particular stream of consciousness" that flows through the life process; a non-autonomous aspect of the Whole. But if we aren't an individuating Soul self, why do we have such a definite causal relationship with our past lives?

Why did I have such an antipathy for the British aristocracy if I did not loath that "foul beast of honor and deceit" in my former lifetime in high society London, England? And if I didn't have a lifetime as a black slave in Georgia, USA why when Penny and went to a spiritual seminar in St. Louis did I have such an affinity for the black people there, whom I felt in the deepest part of my soul were "my people"? And even more personal still, why did I have such an unnatural attraction for older women in my current lifetime if it wasn't for what I did to them in my morally and sexually depraved lifetime as *"le salaud de Paris"* in the mid-17th Century? And if I had not dishonored our family honor with my mistress, do you think I would have been so attracted to Penny who was my wife la Dona Francesca in Genoa, Italy? My attraction to Penny was so karmically powerful that it mystified me for years until I had my seven past-life regressions. This is why past-life regression therapy is so effective and popular today; because it goes a long way to explaining why we are the way we are, and why we are with the people we're with...

"There is no other approach that I have experienced, or seen, as effective as past-life therapy in getting people through lifelong, and

maybe multiple lives of problems," said the "Father of Holistic Medicine" Dr. Norman Shealy "Why?" he asked Past Life Therapist Morris Netherton, Ph.D., who replied: "Norm, it lets the human mind lift its boundaries and look wherever it needs to look to find solutions for whatever bothers you. And it's a very simple process if you see it being done…" (You Tube interview: *The Power of Past Lives*).

When Dr. Brian Weiss asked his patient Catherine to go back to the time when her problem began, she didn't go back to her childhood as he expected; she went back to a past lifetime, as does every person seeking past-life regression therapy. And if this doesn't prove the continuity of the individuation of our Soul self from one life to the next, I don't know what does; so again I ask, how did this Buddhist notion of the *non-self* get such a firm grip on the psyche of man? Why does this notion that is so counter-intuitive to what Carl Jung called "the true *spiritus rector* of all biological and psychic events" persist?

The only explanation that I can offer was inspired by something that Gurdjieff said to his inner circle of students. Like Socrates, Gurdjieff also employed the analogy of prison to illustrate man's situation in life. "He must first of all realize that he is in prison," said Gurdjieff; "Further, no one can escape from prison without the help of those who have escaped before. Only they can say in what way escape is possible or can send tools, files, or whatever may be necessary…" (*In Search of the Miraculous*, p. 30).

Gurdjieff also said something else about man's prison. Unfortunately, I can't recall where I read it; but he compared man's prison to a very large complex with many rooms. A prisoner in one room may escape to a larger room and think that he has escaped from his prison, but he has only escaped to a much larger room of the same prison complex; and that's what I feel the Buddhists have done with their notion of the *non-self*: they have escaped from the prison of their own mind into the infinitely large room of the Mental Plane of Consciousness characterized by *non-being*, or NOTHINGNESS.

And when one escapes from the prison of his own mind and centers himself in the NOTHINGNESS of his *non-being*, like Krishnamurti, he will have no personal center. This is why H. P. Blavatsky wrote in *The Voice of the Silence*: "The Mind is the great Slayer of the Real. Let the Disciple slay the Slayer."

DO WE HAVE AN IMMORTAL SOUL?

Mercifully, escape is still possible; because if we don't get it right in this life, we will just keep coming back until we do...

38. Sinatra's Signature Song

The secret code of our life. If we want to escape from the prison of our own mind, we have to discover the secret code of our life; which David Whyte was called to do when the *Trickster* woke him up to himself by having him unconsciously ask the question that locked its talons into his soul and refused to let him go.

I have no doubt that the sheer humiliation of his question had the same effect on him as the question *"Why do you lie?"* had upon me; and like me, David Whyte had to take up the quest for his lost soul because he really had no choice.

As I said, the Way is the Way is the Way; but the Way is an individual path, and the only entry point into the mysteries of the inherently self-transcending miracle of the Way is one's own *karmic destiny*. And David Whyte's *karmic destiny* was *the poet's way*, just as painting was *the artist's way* for Canadian artist Robert Bateman.

Robert Bateman was an abstract artist, which was the trend in modern art at the time; and he worked at abstract painting until he could get no more out of it. One day he stood back from his last abstract painting and studied it. *"Is that it?"* he asked himself. *"Is that all there is to art?"* His heart sank, and he fell into a state of depression.

Then the merciful law of divine synchronicity came into play, as it always does when one comes to a spiritual impasse in their life. Robert was "inspired" to go to Buffalo, New York to take in an art show by the American realist painter Andrew Wyeth.

Robert studied Andrew Wyeth's natural landscapes which so resonated with him that he had an epiphany that he compared to St. Paul's road to Damascus revelation. *"I found my way!"* he exclaimed, and he reconnected with his "inner artist" and went on to become Canada's most famous wildlife artist. And, as often happens when one has been smitten by the inherently reconciling spirit of the Way, he also became an active environmentalist.

DO WE HAVE AN IMMORTAL SOUL?

"I found my way!" What did Robert Bateman mean by that? What did Frank Sinatra mean when he sang his signature song "My Way" that resonated with so many people across the world? Few people know it, but "My Way" has an interesting history.

The lyrics were written by Canadian singer Paul Anka, which he set to music based upon the original 1967 French pop song *Comme d'habitude* (As Usual) to which he had acquired publishing rights; and it tells the story of a man who, having grown old, reflects on his life as death approaches. He's comfortable with his morality and takes responsibility for how he dealt with all the challenges of his life while maintaining a respectable degree of integrity; and, if I may, I'd like to quote the lyrics because they speak to everyone who dares to take the road less travelled to live their own life:

My Way

And now, the end is near;
And so I face the final curtain.
My friend, I say it clear,
I'll state my case, of which I'm certain.

I've lived a life that's full,
I've travelled each and ev'ry highway;
But more, much more than this,
I did it my way.

Regrets, I've had a few;
But then again, too few to mention.
I did what I had to do
And saw it through without exception.

I planned each charted course;
Each careful step along the byway,
But more, much more than this,
I did it my way.

Yes, there were times, I'm sure you know
When I bit off more than I could chew.

But through it all, when there was doubt,
I ate it up and spit it out.
I faced it all and I stood tall;
And did it my way.

I've loved, I've laughed and cried.
I've had my fill; my share of losing.
And now, as tears subside,
I find it all so amusing.

To think I did all that;
And may I say—not in a shy way,
"No, oh no not me,
I did it my way."

For what is man, what has he got?
If not himself, then he has naught.
To say the things he truly feels;
And not the words of one who kneels.
The record shows I took the blows—
And did it my way!

My high school hero Larry Darrel, the wandering soul in Maugham's novel *The Razor's Edge*, gave up a promising conventional life of marriage and professional security to be true to his spiritual calling; and Carl Jung risked his sanity by daring to "confront the unconscious," which he recorded in what has become the best known record of *the hero's journey;* and Jerry Wennstrom burnt all his artwork and gave away his possessions to forge a new path entirely conditional upon the "Universe" taking care of him; and David Whyte was severed from the security of his profession to take up *the poet's way* as I was severed from mine to look for my lost soul, just as every person in the world who can no longer bear to suffer the *unbearable longing* for "wholeness and singleness of self" steps into the unknown to live the life that their *karmic destiny* calls for them to live—that's what the song "My Way" speaks to, the courage that it takes to be true to one's calling.

Doing it "my way" is the secret code of our life...

39. My Royal Flush

Once again, man's natural impulse to individuate his *core self* that is reflected in the two key lines of "My Way" belie the Buddhist notion of the *non-self*: **"For what is man, what has he got? /If not himself, then he is naught."** Which points to the reality of our greatest need—to satisfy our inherent longing (unbearable or not) for "wholeness and singleness of self." Having said this, I feel called upon now to finally show my hand…

I certainly didn't expect to get it, but I favored the odds by taking evolution into my own hands by living the Way *consciously* with Gurdjieff's teaching, my *Royal Dictum*, the sayings of Jesus, and dozens of careful chosen wisdom sayings; and after giving birth to my spiritual self I grew in my own "wholeness and singleness of self" until I was privileged to catch a glimpse into the Divine Plan of God, thereby granting me the best possible hand in the poker game of life—*a Royal Flush in Hearts.*

One needs a *Royal Flush in Hearts* to answer Gauguin's famous three questions, "Where do we come from? What are we? Where are we going?" But because we are the authors of our own *karmic destiny*, we always get the hand that we deserve; that's why I experienced what I did in my fourth past-life regression. So, no more dancing around the mulberry bush; whether one believes me or not, this is the hand that I was dealt…

Like my experience in the back yard of our family home thirty years earlier when I went back through time to experience the genesis of life on Planet Earth, in my fourth past-life regression I went even further back—all the way back to where I had come from before I had even realized the consciousness of my reflective self: *I went all the way back to the Body of God, that Great Ocean of Love and Mercy where all atoms of God come from.*

I was an atom of God in the Body of God, but I had so self-consciousness. I had Soul consciousness, but no reflective self-consciousness; and the only way I knew this was because I was an evolved self-realized Soul self when I experienced myself in the Body of God before I was sent into the lower worlds to evolve into a self-realized Soul self.

If you will, in my regression I experienced the dual consciousness of my un-self-realized soul and my self-realized Soul self; that's how I came to experience that I was an atom of God in the Body of God. *And I cannot describe how blissful this was.*

But something was missing. That's why I was sent into the lower worlds to grow and evolve and constellate the consciousness of life, starting at the very inception of life on Planet Earth (*which I had already experienced thirty years earlier!*) through all the various life forms until my individuating soul had constellated enough consciousness of life to reach critical mass in a higher evolved species and become aware of itself as an individual *I am unit of consciousness*, and which I was also granted the privilege of experiencing.

After I was sent from the Body of God into the lower worlds, I experienced my evolution up the chain of life from its inception all the way up to the species of primordial man, an anthropoid creature; and I was the alpha male of a group of ten or twelve of these higher primates. I did not have self-consciousness yet; but I experienced myself as a very brutish creature that governed its clan members with brutal beatings and what in my novel *Cathedral of My Past Lives* I came to call "power grunts."

I grunted all the time to invoke fear. That's how I kept my clan members in check (and also to appropriate the consciousness of their will-to-be that fed my individuation, which speaks to man's primal need to control and dominate); so, for literary purposes, I called myself "Grunt" in my first primordial human life. And when I had experienced myself long enough as "Grunt" in my regression to see that I did not have a reflective self, I was brought to that actual moment in time when I gave birth to my reflective self!

As incredible as this was, **I actually experienced the dawning of a new "I" of God, and I became a self-aware Soul self!** I was only dimly aware of myself, mind you; but enough to set me apart from the group consciousness of my clan. And, believe me, this separation filled me with so much fear, anxiety, and dread that I cannot describe it; which leads me to make a point here about something that Jesus said to Glenda Green:

*"You see, the point of my sacrifice on the cross does not lie so much in the fact that I died for you as that I **separated for you**. Death means nothing for me, for I am utterly assured of my immortality and the pain of death could have been cancelled in a moment by my love. My gift to mankind was the separation that I **chose** to experience. Uniformly without exception, the separations of man have occurred because man **drifted away** from God, the Source of love and reality, through his devotion to private fiction and ego projections. Man's headlong pursuit of personal agendas and invented realities cause him to forget the love that he is. **I separated as an act of love**, so that love could then be united even with the act of separation. The long estrangement from God could then be ended"* (Love without End, Jesus Speaks, pp. 339-40).

Jesus sacrificed his life on the cross to reconnect us with God through love, the bridge that will connect us from our separation from God—**if we so choose**. Jesus continues:

*"The miracle evoked by my death was the cancellation of separation **by equating it with love instead of judgment.** The miracle of my resurrection is not so much that my body was made whole **as that man was made whole with God,** and separation was transmuted to an illusion. This transfiguration is now available to anyone who accepts the love that he is. You may perpetuate the illusion if you choose, or you may accept the gift. This was my Father's gift and mine, given freely to anyone who wishes to regard the change of potential which now exists for mankind"* (Ibid. p. 340).

It took a long time to part the veil of life, but I finally saw through the mystery of the Divine Plan of God: **our separation from God was necessary**; because through the process of life, the un-self-realized atoms of God (Soul seeds, if you will) evolve through life for the divine purpose of individuating the consciousness of God so that God can grow in the consciousness of God. As Meister Eckart said: *"God is not blessed in his Godhead. He must be born in man* *forever."* This is why Paul Twitchell said, "Man is as important to God as God is to man." We exist in a symbiotic relationship with God, and no soul is more relevant than any other in the Divine Plan of God. We are all equal; and the only difference is in the degree of our self-realization, which is the premise of our *karmic destiny...*

Finally, I was dealt the missing pieces to the puzzle of life; and my experience as an un-self-realized atom of God in the Body of God and birth of my reflective self, which, along with the other three pieces that I had already been dealt—my experience of the inception of life on Planet Earth, my self-initiation into the inherently self-transcending miracle of the Way, and the birth of my spiritual self—gave me the five cards of my *Royal Flush* that finally solved the mystery of life:

> Question: *Where do we come from?*
> Answer: God.
> Question: *What are we?*
> Answer: Atoms of God.
> Question: *Where are we going?*
> Answer: Back to God.

But I didn't piece the puzzle together until I wrote my novel *Cathedral of My Past Lives*, because I needed the inherent genius of my creative unconscious to put the pieces together into a recognizable whole. Apart, each incredible experience stood dreadfully alone and impenetrable; but together they joyfully solved the puzzle of life.

And the beautiful thing about my *Royal Flush in Hearts* was that it didn't come from my own mind, which I could never trust; it came from the daily experiences of my personal path, which was driven by the noble virtue of **Goodness**.

That's why I have no doubt of the certainty of my answer, which puts the lie to the spiritually offensive cerebral notion of the *non-self*. But as certain as I was, I still had a lot of creative writing to do before I understood my answer...

40. And that's how I "Pulled it off"

From the moment I gave birth to my reflective self in my first primordial human life, I began to create personal karma. I had a reflective self now, and as rudimentary as it was I was now making personal choices because I was aware of my separateness from my clan, and all of life actually; and thus began the individuation process of my *core self*.

My *core self* was my Soul self, a newborn "I" of God; and from lifetime to lifetime I created personal karma that fueled the individuation process of my *core self*. Creating karma is nature's way of gathering and constellating the life force that our *core self* needs to grow and evolve in the consciousness of God; but it took me a long time to make the connection that the consciousness of life *is* the consciousness of God.

When I slipped into the amino acids that made up the first building blocks of life in my totally unexpected experience that sunny spring day in the back yard of our family home thirty years before I had my past-life regressions, I *knew* that I had just *animated* the life process on Planet Earth; but it took my regression to the Body of God and the dawning of my reflective self for me to see that what initiated the life process was not me *per se*, but Soul consciousness—meaning, the *I Am* consciousness of God!

Because I was an evolved self-realized Soul self that experienced the inception of life on earth, I was confused as to how I could be responsible for the genesis of life; and not until I experienced myself as an un-self-realized atom of God in the Body of God that was sent into the lower worlds to evolve through the life process and give birth to a new "I" of God did I finally connect the dots and realize that it wasn't me personally that was responsible for jump-starting the life process, but the un-self-realized *I Am* consciousness of God; and it is this *I Am* consciousness of God that seeks total self-realization—or God Realization Consciousness, if you will. This is what constitutes our spiritual destiny.

And at the risk of repetition, this is precisely what Carl Jung intuited when he wrote in *Memories, Dreams, Reflections*: "Unconscious wholeness therefore seems to be the true *spiritus rector* of all biological and psychic events. Here is a principle which strives for total realization—which in man's case signifies the attainment of total consciousness. Attainment of consciousness is culture in the broadest sense, and self-knowledge is therefore the heart and essence of this process. The Oriental attributes unquestionably divine significance to the self, and according to ancient Christian (Gnostic) view self-knowledge is the road to knowledge of God. The decisive question for man is*: Is he related to something infinite or not? That is the telling question of his life*" (pp. 324-5, italics mine).

This "principle which strives for total realization" is the atom of God, the individuating consciousness of Soul, the un-self-realized *I Am* consciousness of God which in man's case is our Soul self. This is why when Moses asked the voice in the burning bush to identify itself it said, "I Am THAT I Am"—because God both *is* and is *becoming*. This is the mystery that I was privileged to resolve with the *Royal Flush* that I was dealt…

"Man must finish the work which nature left incomplete" said the Alchemists, whose secret teaching taught one how to accomplish this task; but what they could not explain was why nature could not complete the individuation of our Soul self.

Nature is governed by laws. Perhaps one day the new science of *quantum spirituality* that adventurous souls like Dr. Amit Goswami is exploring will recognize that the spiritual laws of karma and reincarnation are not spiritual laws at all, but natural laws that drive the individuation process of life; but whether they are spiritual or natural laws, it does not matter because to complete the individuation of our Soul self we have to take responsibility for our own karma. This is the only way we can transcend ourselves and complete what nature cannot finish; because karma and reincarnation keep us bound to nature's eternal process of *being* and *becoming*; or life and death, if you will.

I wouldn't know this if I hadn't experienced it. I transcended the consciousness of my *being* and *non-being* and gave birth to my spiritual self, which can better be explained by saying that I shifted my center of gravity (my "I" consciousness) from my lower self (my human ego personality) to my higher self (my individuating Soul self), and I became a spiritually self-realized Soul—or, if you will, I realized "wholeness and singleness of self" just as Jesus promised if one lived his sayings and made the two into one. That's why I could write in my journal: *I am what I am not, and I am not what I am; I am both, but neither: I am Soul.* This is what the Alchemists sought to accomplish.

Still, I have not quite explained how I "pulled it off," have I?

Gary Zukav intuited the process when he said to Lilou Mace when she interviewed him for her *Juicy Living Tour Interviews*, "You have to align your personality with soul," which I came to recognize as the alignment of our personal *karmic destiny* with our pre-scripted *spiritual destiny*. So, how does one do this? More specifically, how did I do it?

By creating the *right kind of personality*; a personality that is inherently self-transcending—the kind of personality that the poets have intuited with the genius of their gift to "transform reality into a deeper perception of what is," as the American poet Adrienne Rich expressed it. And this *"deeper perception of what is"* is the Way, the omniscient guiding force of life that UNDERLIES and DEFINES the human condition.

The Irish poet Seamus Heaney alludes to this process of *"transforming reality into a deeper perception of what is"* when he delivered his Nobel Lecture in Stockholm upon receiving the 1995 Nobel Prize for Literature:

"...what the necessary poetry always does, which is to touch the base of our sympathetic nature while taking in at the same time the unsympathetic nature of the world to which that nature is constantly exposed. The form of the poem, in other words, is crucial to poetry's power to do the thing which always is and always will be to poetry's credit: **the power to persuade that vulnerable part of our consciousness of its rightness in spite of the evidence of wrongness all around it, the power to remind us that we are hunters and gatherers of values**, that our very solitudes and distresses are creditable, in so far as they, too, are an earnest of our veritable human being" (bold italics mine).

The poet's genius recognizes that we have to reconcile the good with the bad in human nature, that we have to make the two into one by "hunting and gathering" those values that transform our nature and make us whole. This is what Twitchell meant when he said that ***spirituality cannot be taught but must be caught.*** And this is precisely what I learned to do as I lived Gurdjieff's most secret teaching, "the way of the sly man."

I can only describe "the way of the sly man" as the path of spiritual survival in the unforgiving jungle of life. This is the path of "catching spirit" in one's daily interactions with the negative forces of life. This is the path of learning how to recognize how life seeks to compromise you of your integrity when you least expect it, and of learning how to skillfully thwart life's efforts; which I learned how to do so well that it inspired my second volume of spiritual musings— *Old Whore Life, Exploring the Shadow Side of Karma.*

I saw life as an "old whore that screwed me of my virtue," but it took a long time for me to acknowledge the shocking truth that I was "old whore life" and that I screwed myself of my own virtue, and the only way that I would ever reconcile my *unconscious shadow* (my unresolved karmic self) with my *conscious personality* was to transform the blind, selfish consciousness of my "old whore self" by living by a set of transformative values that were inherently self-transcending—like the noble virtues, for example.

And I made conscious, concerted, and relentless efforts to forge into a personal ethic the five noble virtues of **HONESTY**, **FAIRNESS**, **COMPASSION**, **FORGIVENESS**, and my favorite virtue **GOODNESS** which Socrates deemed to be the most noble.

Following my favorite poet William Wordsworth's advice from "Character of the Happy Warrior," which became my ideal, I did my utmost to **"labor good on good to fix"** to transform the consciousness of my *shadow self* and become whole; that's how I created *the right kind of personality* that aligned my *karmic destiny* with my *spiritual destiny* until my two destinies become one path which I'm proud to call, ***"My Way."*** And that's how I "pulled it off."

Orest Stocco,
Georgian Bay, Ontario
Dec. 25, 2013

OTHER BOOKS BY OREST STOCCO

Stupidity Is Not a Gift of God
Spiritual Musings – Volume 3

Tea with Grace
A Story of Synchronicity and Platonic Love

Letters to Padre Pio

Jesus Wears Dockers,
The Gospel Conspiracy Story

Old Whore Life
Exploring the Shadow Side of Karma

Healing with Padre Pio

Why Bother?
The Riddle of the Good Samaritan

Just Going With the Flow
And Other Spiritual Musings

Keeper of the Flame

My Unborn Child

What Would I Say Today If I Were To Die Tomorrow?
Reflections on the Life of a Seeker

On the Wings of Habitat
A Volunteer's Story

ABOUT THE AUTHOR

Orest Stocco was born in Panettieri, Calabria, Italy. He immigrated to Canada and studied philosophy at university. A student of Gurdjieff's teaching for many years which opened him up to the Way, his passion for writing inspired such works as *Stupidity Is Not a Gift of God* and *Healing with Padre Pio*. He lives in Georgian Bay, Ontario with his life mate Penny Lynn Cates. His personal dictum is: life is an individual journey.

Visit him at: http://www.oreststocco.com

Spiritual Musings Blog:

http://www.spiritualmusingsbyoreststocco.blogspot.com

ME AND MY SISPHYEAN ROCK

www.ingramcontent.com/pod-product-compliance
Lightning Source LLC
Chambersburg PA
CBHW051832040426

42447CB00006B/486